The
Works
of
Mercy:
New
Perspectives
on
Ministry

The Works of Mercy: New Perspectives on Ministry

Francis A. Eigo, O.S.A.
Editor

The Villanova University Press

Copyright © 1992 by Francis A. Eigo, O.S.A.
The Villanova University Press
Villanova, Pennsylvania 19085
Library of Congress Cataloging-in-Publication Data
The Works of mercy: new perspectives on ministry / Francis A. Eigo,
editor.

p.   cm.
Includes index.
ISBN 0-87723-083-8
1. Corporal works of mercy. I. Eigo, Francis A.
BV4647.M4W67 1991
253 — dc20   91-46483
                                                        CIP

To
All
Sisters
of
Mercy:
Past,

Present,

Future

Contents

Contributors

SIDNEY CALLAHAN, professor of psychology at Mercy College, Dobbs Ferry, New York, is the recipient of many honors, has held a number of academic positions, and has been involved in a variety of professional activities, especially as the author of numerous essays, columns, articles, and books, including such works as *Conscience Reconsidered: Reason and Emotion in Moral Decision Making,* the prizewinning *With All Our Heart and Mind: The Spiritual Works of Mercy in a Psychological Age,* and as the coeditor of *Abortion: Understanding Differences.*

FRANCIS SCHÜSSLER FIORENZA, Charles Chauncey Stillman Professor of Roman Catholic Theological Studies at Harvard University Divinity School, is the coeditor of *Systematic Theology: Catholic Perspectives,* a two volume compendium of Roman Catholic Systematic Theology, and the author of more than seventy-five essays, published in scholarly journals, one hundred twenty-five book reviews, and a number of books, including the prizewinning *Foundational Theology: Jesus and the Church.*

PETER R. GATHJE, a member of the Open Door Community of Atlanta, Georgia, has been engaged in a number of scholarly activities: University, college, high school teaching; recipient of a number of academic honors; author of essays, book reviews, and the recently published book, *Christ Comes in the Stranger's Guise.*

DORIS GOTTEMOELLER, R.S.M., currently President of the Sisters of Mercy of the Americas, has taught at all levels, served on numerous health and educational boards, lectured widely, published in journals and magazines, edited *Women and Ministry: Present Experience and Future Hopes,* and authored *Catholic Health Ministry: A New Vision for a New Century.*

GERALD A. McHUGH, JR., member of the Pennsylvania Bar and Bars of the United States District Court, and the Third Circuit Court of Appeals, is the recipient of numerous honors, has lectured widely, is deeply involved in many community service activities, and is the author of reports, articles for professional journals, book reviews, and books, including *Christian Faith and Criminal Justice: Toward a Christian Response to Crime and Punishment.*

SUZANNE C. TOTON, a member of the faculty of Villanova University, has authored a number of articles for journals and magazines, chapters for scholarly books, the award winning *World Hunger: The Responsibility of Christian Education* as well as the forthcoming *Educating Toward a Politically Responsible Church.*

Introduction

After some general perspectives (Sidney Callahan's essay) and theological perspectives (Francis Schüssler Fiorenza's) on the works of mercy, this twenty-fourth volume of the *Proceedings of the Theology Institute of Villanova University* focuses on four specific works of mercy and some new perspectives on ministering them: feeding the hungry (Suzanne C. Toton), housing the homeless (Peter R. Gathje), ransoming the captive (Gerald A. McHugh, Jr.), and visiting the sick (Doris Gottemoeller).

Once again, I am most grateful to the members of the Theology Institute Committee (Walter Conn, Edward Hamel, O.S.A., Bernard Lazor, O.S.A., Thomas Ommen, Suzanne Toton) who assisted me in the planning and execution stages of my work as Director of the Theology Institute, to Patricia Fry who assisted me in the production of this volume, to all the essayists who made such a tremendous contribution, and to the administrators of Villanova University who made all of this possible.

Francis A. Eigo, O.S.A.
Editor

The Works of Mercy: General Perspectives

Sidney Callahan

What are the works of mercy? Who can perform them? To whom are they directed and why? How are they carried out? These simple questions need answers, but the analyses and explorations required have hardly begun. Even so, the Catholic Church, undeterred by less than full clarity and comprehension, has, century after century, confidently listed fourteen works of mercy which the faithful are enjoined to perform in the pursuit of salvation. These acts are considered central to Christian living, even if they are vaguely defined and poorly understood.

The ability to practice what is not fully analyzed or articulated is characteristic of individuals and of individual cultures in the process of growth. Piaget, the great developmental psychologist, pointed out that children can often learn to do things and perform operations that they can not describe. They cannot yet articulate, or even self-consciously know, that they know how to perform. There is a difference between knowing *how* and knowing *that* one knows how. In the same way, the Church, in its tradition, can be seen to continually preserve elements which are yet to be fully examined. The works of mercy are an example of a carefully preserved treasure of the Catholic heritage which has been more or less left unanalyzed.[1]

I approach the traditional works of mercy from a general and psychological perspective, with certain basic questions. Definitions are in order, along with a need to examine the underlying assumptions concerning the nature of human persons and the nature of interpersonal relationships that undergird the idea of works of mercy. This exploration comes down to the familiar questions of what, why, who, and how?

1

What are the works of mercy?

A work of mercy, if it is to be a work, must be a conscious, intentional action directed to an end. Obviously, machines, insects, newborn infants or unconscious adults can not act at a level of coherent purposefulness. Reflexive actions or instinctual responses would hardly qualify as an organized operation to achieve an end. A certain level of consciousness and goal orientation is necessary for any act which can be defined as "work." Only humans work in the full sense of the word.[2] Humans alone know that they are acting according to a purposeful plan, focusing and adapting their efforts to do whatever it takes to accomplish the envisioned end.

A work of mercy requires a kind of knowing—a consciousness of intention and purposefulness—and a sense of self, able to interact with another or others. An agent must aim at meeting a need in an effective way. Therefore, there must be a practical knowledge of the other and of the concrete situation. There must be an accurate perception of a need or deficit of some kind which can be possible only if there is a recognition of what fulfillment or plenitude would be like. There has to be a further recognition that the self as agent can purposefully act to help meet the need or correct the deficit. A decision must be made to act—a decision which is not purely reflexive or physically coerced. The decision can be a long deliberated, self-reflective act or an almost instantaneous move. But, the motivation for meeting the need must be of a particular kind.

The motive for a work of mercy is to act mercifully. Mercy is defined as compassion, kindness, benevolence, as found in acts of good will or unselfish love. Mercy is also defined as forbearance, as when a judge does not impose a penalty, or one who holds power over others does not harm them or lets them off. This part of the definition emphasizes that mercy is free or gratuitous, something more than what could be exacted by legal coercion or legal norms. A work of mercy is an act of compassionate kindness which is also merciful in that it is freely undertaken and uncoerced. The fourteen works of mercy which have been handed down in Christian tradition make it clear that these are acts of uncoerced benevolence. The seven corporal works of mercy have been listed as:

> To feed the hungry,
> To give drink to the thirsty,
> To clothe the naked,
> To shelter the homeless,
> To visit the sick,

To visit those in prison or ransom the captive,
To bury the dead.

The spiritual works of mercy have been listed as:

To admonish the sinner,
To instruct the ignorant,
To counsel the doubtful,
To comfort the sorrowful,
To bear wrongs patiently,
To forgive all injuries,
To pray for the living and the dead.

All of these are acts done by a human agent, directed to meeting the needs of others. Traditionally, the list has been divided into meeting corporal or bodily needs and spiritual needs. Today, we understand that we humans exist as a body/mind unity, so we would not make such a strict division between the two kinds of needs. Obviously, those who have material and physical needs also must have psychological dimensions to their plight or conditions which must be respected and benevolently addressed.

However, it is still the case that there can be a distinction drawn between a human being's illness or physical needs and psychological or spiritual ills. We know we are our bodies, but we are also more than our bodily selves. A person may have all material and physical needs met, and still be suffering or be in need. In affluent America, we regularly see well fed, well cared for, materially secure, talented people damaging themselves in subtle and not so subtle ways. Despair, leading to suicide and drug use, for instance, is epidemic in the population.

Individuals can have needs that they do not consciously feel. The malnourished, those dying from lack of oxygen, and persons with certain dangerous diseases, like hypertension, may not feel any symptoms — no more than do those mired in ignorance or those mindlessly or habitually enmeshed in some oppressive social system always recognize their deficits. Those who sin or injure others may have spiritual or moral needs that they vigorously attempt to deny or suppress. Benevolence toward others must go beyond obvious material needs, or needs of the moment, and attend to longterm needs. The healthy, wealthy, favored children of the world can also need help.

Are there other needs and other benevolent acts of mercy which are not found on the traditional lists? Can love in action find forms other than these works of mercy? Surely the answer is yes. The world always changes, and perhaps the presence of technology alone might produce some additions to both lists, such as to give access to medical healthcare to the poor, or let the dying die humanely without becoming victims of excessive technological treatment. More to the point, today's interpretations of the way to carry out the works of mercy will be various and changing, given the variety of cultures and social conditions that exist today.

Many Christians may find the traditional works of mercy more of an inspiration or initial impetus for work aimed at meeting human needs through structural change and community reorganization. The works of mercy often have been interpreted as one-on-one actions, but other modes of communal corporate operation can and should apply. Groups and institutions, by working together over time, can accomplish more help for whole communities in need than individuals can hope to with an individual by individual approach.

Today, we are acutely aware of the way that social forces, the media, economics, and law shape individual lives. It is important work to struggle against sinful structures, either as a member of a church body or of a corporate group dedicated to justice and reform. An exercise of compassion devoted to reforming unjust structures will usually require knowledge and expertise, since it may not be obvious to the uninitiated the way an oppressive system maintains itself — or what can be done to change things for the better. Individuals and groups do well to prepare themselves to fight for social justice; justice is a basic, minimal constituent of love of neighbor. Those in the community who do not have the expertise to take leadership roles in a struggle for justice can support the initiatives for reform in their neighborhood, state, country, or international community.

The traditional lists of the works of mercy can be seen as a crystallization of human needs which always and everywhere exist and need to be met by corporate groups and by individuals. I will leave the important discussion of corporate modes of carrying out the works of mercy to others. Here, I will explore one to one relationships of compassion between persons; these are worth analyzing in detail since this is an aspect of life no one ever leaves behind. Always and everywhere Christians must live with, and meet the needs of, the individuals they encounter in their daily lives.

Clearly, it has been far easier for today's Christian community to remember and strive to apply the corporal works of mercy more than the spiritual works of mercy. Religious people who have memorized the works of mercy in religious education classes can remember a few of the corporal works, but the spiritual works are often forgotten. They seem to be fast fading from the collective consciousness of the community. Of course, the corporal works of mercy are so dramatically highlighted in the familiar story of the Last Judgment in Matthew 25:34-40, the searing scene in which Jesus asserts that feeding the hungry and clothing the naked and other deeds are actions done to him — just as ignoring those needs were failures to care for the Lord himself.

No such condensed dramatic narrative teaches the list of the spiritual works of mercy. While the directives to counsel, admonish, forgive, pray, and comfort one another are repeatedly enjoined and modelled in Scripture, they are not so concisely delineated in one dramatic image. It is also not easy to determine when the formulation of the list of spiritual works of mercy enters the tradition. And, why have they been presented in the traditional order? I have wondered whether the order given symbolizes a progression through the life cycle or through increasing degrees of difficulty? Surely, the last listed, to pray for the living and the dead, is an action that requires the most faith in the new order of the Kingdom and may be the most difficult to practice.

Visibility of a need and visibility of consequences of an act make it easier to do. Perhaps the overt concreteness of the corporal works of mercy helps them remain dominant in the consciousness of the faithful. The body and its needs remain much the same wherever and whenever one lives, whether in Galilee, fifth century Rome, medieval France, or on the lower East Side of New York. Houses of Hospitality, founded by Dorothy Day's Catholic Worker Movement, preach the works of mercy and continue to feed, clothe, and shelter those in need, with love and respect. Mother Teresa began her mission by picking up one dying person off the street to give him care and comfort. Everyone who lives needs food, water, shelter, and care when illness, imprisonment, or death strikes. We know what to do when we see a clear bodily need. There is no disagreement between donor and recipient as to what will serve the person. Those who are hungry, thirsty, and homeless clearly want food, water, and shelter. But, few sinners want to be admonished, and the ignorant do not always seek to be instructed.

Meeting psychological and spiritual needs of another person is a more problematic proposition. Inner worlds of individuals change over time and can differ from culture to culture and from era to era. Cultural evolution takes place at a more rapid rate than the biological evolution which has produced the human body. While there are always psychosocial constants in human life, else we could not understand or be moved by the plays

of Sophocles or Shakespeare, psychological and social visions of
the meaning of human beings and human relationships change.
Efforts to meet spiritual needs are going to be different in different cultural settings, when a person's beliefs, worldviews, and
standards of appropriate behavior vary.

The concept of a person and what constitutes an individual
self may differ from era to era. Whatever efforts at communication worked well in Rome, or in medieval periods, or in Victorian eras, may not be effective today. Consider the different
expectations modern persons living in democracies have for
their right to be treated fairly and justly in social interactions—
a different expectation from that in societies in which class, gen-
der, and inherited privileges were assumed to prevail. Our ideas
about the role of women, men, children, education, and government have changed. More centrally, concepts of the will or
individual freedom or of an appropriate display of grief or emotional bonding may differ.

I think that, as technology has increased, human beings have
in reaction emphasized, or perhaps been forced to recognize,
human subjectivity and consciousness. There has been a turn
to the interior and psychological awareness which makes persons more aware of their individual perspectives, reactions, and
worldviews. In our own modern pluralistic society, we know
that different personal understandings can coexist on many important matters: human life, sex, family, death, and what constitutes a need, as opposed to a desire. When perspectives,
ideals, and expectations differ from person to person, any communication or psychological interaction becomes a subtle challenge.

In the spiritual works of mercy, we see psychological efforts,
on the part of a conscious person, directed to the consciousness
of another person or persons. Admonishing, instructing, counseling, comforting, bearing patiently, forgiving, and praying for
another, all are person focused acts of personally engaged self-
consciousness. I assume here that personal actions can include
more than overt motor or verbal speech acts.

Individual selves can act in covert, internal ways; human beings can engage in voluntary acts of reasoning, feeling, imagining, remembering, reflecting, and willing. We may not be able
to visibly observe interior acts of consciousness, but they are
taking place. Of course, if we had persons wired up or in various brain imaging scanners, we could see the traces and images
of the brain's mental activity. At least, the ghost of consciousness is visible through modern technology.

Personal consciousness is partly a spontaneous stream of thoughts, images, and feelings that involuntarily emerge into the mind and partly those acts of consciousness that individuals purposefully direct and enact.[3] While persons are awake and alert, they can voluntarily direct, focus, and engender their consciousness to think or imagine or feel in certain ways. The spiritual works of mercy are directed personal acts of thinking, feeling, and communicating with, and for, other persons who are also thinking, feeling, and reflective selves. Usually, these acts take place in some face to face interpersonal relationship, although not always. There is no personal contact in some cases, as when communicating by writing or in praying for another who is distant in time or place. But, when we are in direct communication with another, interpersonal contexts and interpersonal responsiveness are crucial to the spiritual works of mercy.

At this point in the discussion, I must confront the meaning and use of the word "spiritual" when used in the spiritual works of mercy. Spiritual refers both to the way the act is performed and to the aim and purpose of the act. I judge that spiritual refers to "spirit" which denotes a person's self consciousness and potential for active thinking, feeling, and willing. In other words, I see "spirit" in this sense as a human psychological capacity or as the all important conscious dimension of a human being.

The human spirit can, I think, be equated to the active consciousness or self, the "I am" of awareness. This self consciousness or "I" thinks, feels, wills, and directs reflection and action. There is more to the human organism, or even to psychological functioning, than the self or spirit, but the spirit or I is what William James called the "self of selves."[4] The active self conscious part of the self differs from those parts of every person's functioning which is automatic, spontaneous, or reflexive. Much of our hard-wired bodily and mental processing, as in perceptual encoding, decoding, and memory retrieval, is so deeply unconscious that it is probably forever outside of our personal knowledge, intervention, or control.[5]

By contrast, our highly aware human consciousness and self consciousness are always accessible while we are awake. Consciousness and our uniquely human self consciousness seem reserved for fairly high levels of processing of our environment. It is most often used in deciding and problem solving. While he/she is alive, awake, and mentally unimpaired, there exists in the mature human being an "I" who is able, not only to receive impressions, but also to direct attention and will action as a free agent.

But, how does this human "spirit," "I am," or "self of selves" relate to the Spirit of God? In faith, we affirm that we are made in the image of God and that God, Christ, and the Holy Spirit reside within us. But, we are also separate creations. The spirit of a human being can be spoken of apart from the divine Spirit with a capital "S," as when Paul says, "The Spirit himself gives witness with our spirit that we are children of God, heirs with Christ . . ." (Rom.8:16). The relationship of the Spirit to the spirit as self conscious "I am" is a theological question of great difficulty and much moment. Answers to this question must also involve the question of what is meant by "the soul." How does the soul relate to the spirit, or to the Spirit?

My own tentative understanding at this point is to see the word "soul" as referring to the reality or form of the whole human organism, existing through time, as fully known to God. The spirit is the active psychological self consciousness or "I," that is known or can be known by myself and others. I believe that the distinct, unique, individual spirit, or self, or "I am" is deeply grounded in God and the Spirit, but the way this indwelling and relationship exist and operate is beyond my comprehension. How exactly do we psychologically meet God within our selves? I do not know, but I think that any simple equating of the Divine with the unconscious is an inadequate solution. We really do not yet understand the nature of the unconscious, despite the assertions of either Freudian or Jungian thinkers.[6]

At this point, all we seem to know is that many believers experience their conscious self awareness to be completely unique, individual, and free, as well as surrounded, buoyed up, led, or in communion with some deeper Reality. The "I am" or individual spirit can freely attend to the Divine Spirit within, as well as freely attend to God in Christ beyond the self when taking part in individual and communal worship and prayer.

The act of attentively orienting or offering the self to God can produce experiences of empowerment — I am enabled to think, feel, and act in loving service of others. I can freely act while at the same time recognize that I am being carried along within the dynamic force of the Divine ocean swell. The power of action is both mine and more than mine. The Scriptural words used to describe this experience are apt: Paul speaks of the way Christ lives in me, the Spirit works through me, or of "him who by the power at work within us is able to accomplish abundantly far more than all we can ask or imagine" (Eph.3:20).

There is a power at work within us which accomplishes things at our free behest, but free action is also experienced as a gift given for the asking or given before the asking. Yet, the individual self has to keep struggling to keep attention focused; persevering in the work of loving attention is not easy or automatic. Karl Rahner has described the curious paradox of "how it is that we beg of God something that we ourselves must do."[7] We have to do deeds freely, sometimes with great effort, but it is also as though we are cooperating with larger forces operating through us. Secular psychologists, investigating optimal functioning, have also noted the curious paradox that the most active individual experiences of focused attention also seem to become subsumed into some larger reality; there are a reciprocal giving and getting within an ongoing flow of experience.[8] This psychological experience of both attending and receiving in one's actions brings us to the question of motivation. Why do we perform benevolent acts?

Why do we perform acts of mercy?

The motivation for merciful action is compassion or benevolent love. A work of mercy is, in essence, love in action, along with the understanding that justice is love's minimum requirement. To work for justice in the case of those who are treated unjustly is surely an act of loving good will. Fortunately, acts of love and benevolence are found in all human groups as an essential part of human nature. The foundation of compassion and benevolence seems to be empathy, or the sensation of directly feeling what another feels. Empathy seems a natural endowment of the human species, found always and everywhere, though different individuals and cultures may either encourage or suppress empathy. So, too, our basic emotional capacities can be shaped by individual choices and cultural socialization.[9]

The human species is so constituted that we have an emotional system that begins to develop in infancy and remains an important dimension in our adult functioning.[10] There are pan-human emotions, complete with recognizable facial expressions and action tendencies which are the same everywhere. The basic emotions are usually seen to consist of joy, guilt, shame, fear, interest, anger, contempt, disgust, and sadness. Love is also universal and seems at first a blend of joy and interest, with a predisposition to approach and value the beloved object or person. Primary emotions become blended and cognitively more elaborated and differentiated in different social psychological environments which provide different experiences. Individuals may also differ in innate temperamental predispositions to certain emotional patterns. Throughout life, emotions interact with our thinking abilities and other actions, and there are three way interactions among thoughts, feeling, and behavior.[11]

Empathy and love appear very early in children who have not been abused or deprived. Small children show altruistic empathy for others.[12] Children have been observed to try to help another in distress. They may try to comfort an adult by bringing him/her their own baby bottle and blanket — not a cognitively sophisticated strategy — but, the motivation to relieve distress is there. I think that a small child or mentally retarded adult could have enough consciousness to try to act compassionately toward others. A decision to act compassionately may be made without the high levels of self consciousness or cognitively elaborate judgments which would make the action more successful.

The effectiveness of a helping action will depend upon the intellectual and human development of the person who acts. With more intellectual development, empathy becomes accompanied by sympathy and love for the other person as he or she exists, with specific needs. These positive emotions and emotionally charged thoughts induce decisions to act benevolently. As the person trying to be compassionate becomes more intelligent and emotionally sensitive to others, his/her acts of mercy can become more skilled, subtle, and effective.

Certain negative emotions also play a role in motivating benevolent acts of helping. Guilt, shame, contempt, and anger over injustice also fuel positive helping actions. When a person fails to help or rejects the opportunity to do something he/she thinks he/she should have done, he/she can feel guilt and shame. He/she can also make amends and resolve to do differently at the next opportunity. A person learns to act benevolently in order to avoid self reproach and guilt.

Another important kind of guilt has also been noted. Empathy, sympathy, and identification with others who are suffering while one's own life is filled with good fortune can produce what has been called "nonmoral guilt," or existential guilt.[13] The person has not been the causal agent in the suffering of others, nor has the person omitted a specific obligated duty. But, the very fact that one has by chance survived, or been born so fortunate, while others less lucky are suffering or have died, produces a feeling of guilt which seeks to restore equity and make reparations for fate's inequalities. A person is impelled to help others in order to right the wrongs of cruel chance and circumstance — even on a worldwide scale. Why should those born into Third

World poverty suffer, while the rich live in wasteful extrava-
gance?

Through many decisions to do the right thing over a long
period of development, an individual can become a person who
has internalized standards of moral responsibility which include
doing good and helping others in need. Such a person identifies
with admired models who live altruistically. For Christians, of
course, Christ and Christ's love are the model. In a highly so-
cialized person, it becomes imperative to live up to one's internalized standards in order to feel self respect. The felt need for
self esteem can motivate acts of benevolence. One desires to
meet a moral obligation or even to go beyond the common
standard of helping behavior; it can be deeply satisfying to do so
and a subtle form of self reward. When this happens, is the person actually being merciful, altruistic, or benevolent to another,
or engaging in a form of self satisfying behavior?

There has been a long debate in both psychology and philosophy about whether altruism is possible. If a person is always
rewarded by the internal moral satisfaction one receives from
oneself for doing the right thing, or even the heroic or magnifi-
cent sacrificial thing, is not this again a form of selfishness or
self aggrandizement? Then again, when a person views another's suffering and empathetically suffers out of fellow-feeling,
is not the merciful alleviation of suffering motivated mainly by
the need to relieve one's own empathic distress? I am helping
you because it will make me feel better no longer to watch you
suffer. So, does not true altruism vanish?

But, if acts of mercy and altruism are so self rewarding, either
by increasing positive self esteem or by removing guilt or empathic suffering, then why does not everyone act in this way all
the time? Obviously, there are times when the cost for helping
another is going to be high. Then, the pain of helping is going
to be much higher than the pain of watching another suffer or
the pain of not living up to one's own moral standards. It is also
the case that there are many other selfish responses which can
be chosen to cope with the challenging demand of another's distress. Persons can turn away from a disturbing scene or even
flee from the painful sight of another's distress. The upsetting
sight of Lazarus lying at the gate can be shut out of the rich
man's vision (and mind) by quickly retreating into the house
and bolting the door.

Through the intellectual abilities humans possess, we can ra-
tionalize away, delay, or defuse a demand to meet another's
need. Metaphorically, this has been expressed as hardening the
heart. It is even possible to turn the upset of seeing others suffer

into anger aimed at the sufferer. We see that persons regularly blame the victim for being in distress—a tactic which defuses the obligation to help. We also tell ourselves that our world is a just world, so bad things happen only to bad people who somehow have deserved them.

But, what of those persons that do not turn away and regularly try to help those in need? I think it is fair and accurate to say that psychological motivations for benevolent action can be mixed. The motivation for altruistic acts can also vary. They can range all the way from existential guilt and joyful gratitude for one's own good fortune to reluctant obedience to an implacable (because internalized) moral command. Many persons help others, feeling it an onerous sacrifice to moral duty. At the same time, there are other cases of almost unconscious, effortless, instantaneous altruism. Persons are regularly reported in the news who risk their lives or risk other dangers to rescue others; they jump into deep waters, rush into burning buildings, fling themselves into runaway cars to rescue children, and so on. Often, the heroic altruists report that they just acted without thinking in response to the emergency.

How much more complex a situation it is when there is more time to count the costs of helping. Yet, even in these more complex conditions when there is time to think of the existing grave dangers, many altruists have seen their actions as the necessary and obvious thing to do. Why risk one's life defying the Nazis? "Why not?," said one rescuer of Jewish children in Poland, who knew the penalties full well, "If someone falls in the street, do you not help him even if there are so many cars that you might get hit?"[14] Although this altruist recognized the serious costs he could incur, it still seemed clear and simple to him—there was really no other way to act.

But, again, it is clear that most people do not go to the rescue of the afflicted or those in need. Altruism cannot be a completely instinctual act, released in emergencies, because so many persons do not help. In every situation of crisis and rescue, there is still some instantaneous personal decision made to answer the demand for help. It is also the case that the person who performs altruistic acts, supposedly without thinking, has indirectly chosen his or her immediate, intuitive act by a buildup of past choices into a habitual response. The altruist of the moment is a person who has been making decisions in the past to respond to the needs of others. Over time, an altruistic self has been created who almost automatically rescues those in need. Given who the person is or, rather, who the person has chosen to become, the altruistic act is only natural. Helping others is now second nature; it is hardly noticed as a conscious decision.

In some fortunate circumstances, the motivation for doing good deeds transcends the category of either selfishness or self-less altruism. The psychologist, Abraham Maslow, coined the word "synergy" to describe the condition in which two persons are both fulfilled through an interaction which becomes greater than the sum of its parts.[15]

Maslow gives as an example a loving father's act of feeding delicious strawberries to his little child who loves strawberries and is having enormous pleasure eating them. But, the father popping the strawberries into his child's mouth is also getting great pleasure in the child's pleasure — much more pleasure than if he were eating the strawberries himself. Now, is this joy-ful feeding a selfish or unselfish act, or perhaps something be-yond either category? In many works of mercy, the giving and the getting are also joyfully fused. Certainly, many Christians have, like Christ, experienced doing God's work as their meat and drink, feeling that it is truly more blessed to give than to receive. "All the way to heaven is heaven," and so on. The joy of giving becomes a way of receiving more joy.

But, there are other times when helping others will be more conscious and deliberate, even painful. Even for the most saintly person, there are some things and sometimes when it can be hard to give. Perhaps the cost of helping is so high that flight, escape, or denial of the demand is desired. This shrink-ing of the self from the need of others can induce a wrenching struggle. I may want to turn away from the sorrowing or the sick and go home, forget everyone else, and read the paper. Or, in more dreadful moments, a person may have to make painful decisions which are a form of dying to self. In rare cases, it can be a question of physically dying if the person decides to do the altruistic deed. Yet, the demand of love, principle, duty, or what believers discern as God's will impels the act. These decisions to act mercifully are not easy or filled with delight. Certainly, Christians have the Agony in the Garden as an example of how hard the call to obedient love can be.

In looking at these different motivations for benevolent action, we can see a pattern. As a self is transformed in develop-ment over time, more and more acts of merciful benevolence become almost automatic or second nature. The person who has grown in love has made so many prior decisions to love and attend to others that many decisions to act benevolently are al-most necessary — embedded in the habitual responses of the person. The decision is either almost unconscious, or there is a

joyful enthusiasm in the doing. But, everyone on the spiritual
journey also meets new and different challenges or new levels of
demand for love in which conscious decisions and mobilization
of attention and will are demanded. Over a lifetime of trying to
love one's neighbor, a person may experience cycles of joyful
ease, stretching struggles, coasting, denial, remobilization, and
renewed struggle. Each individual will meet different challenges of motivation and have a different history of either
growth or decline in loving acts toward others.

Building upon our human nature as empathetic loving creatures, Christians try to grow in compassion. There is no doubt
about the ultimate answer of faith to the question, "why act
mercifully?" God is merciful to us, and we are called to be merciful to others. Christ exemplified mercy and love to all, and, if
we wish to participate in the Divine life, we must open our
selves to the Spirit of mercy and love. Love and mercy are at the
core of the Christian good news. We are to love God and our
neighbor as ourselves. The idea that each human being is our
neighbor, a fellow child of God, filled with the Spirit, motivates
our loving service to one another as though to Christ.

We know the reason we engage in works of mercy, but who
acts and how are is not so simple.

Who acts, and how does one perform a work of mercy?

There are two main issues in thinking of who can perform a
work of mercy. One issue is whether there is a self which is free
enough to take decisive action. I have assumed in my discussion
of the inner active self or spirit that there is such a self, but more
needs to be said. The other interesting issue is whether one can
self consciously engender benevolence or mercy or love by trying.

The self who acts must be free and not determined if it is to
act freely in a merciful way. While there are still strong pockets
of deterministic ideology in science, psychology, and
philosophy — and perhaps in fundamentalist religion, there are
more and more intellectual defenders of human persons as free
agents who can be morally responsible for their actions. Today,
in psychology, there has been a resurgence of interest in consciousness and self direction through thinking, planning, imagining, and self-talk. Even old behaviorists have taken up the
idea of "self-efficacy," wherein the individual's beliefs about being able to cope ensure that a person can change and modify his
or her own behavior.[16]

In looking at the human organism after what has been called "the cognitive revolution" or the "consciousness revolution" in psychology, one clearly sees that there is more going on than bottom up organic functioning or environmental determinism by external forces. There is also top down regulation of the whole organism by means of the self's conscious action.[17] Whatever the mind may turn out to be, something or someone seems to be able to control the organism in carrying out self-determined plans toward self-determined goals.

Today, it is easier to give evidence for the "I" or self posited by the humanistic psychologists who inherited the seminal thinking of William James. James, as I have noted above, felt that the I or innermost self of selves could go out to meet the world, as well as direct to a great extent what appeared in the stream of consciousness. He thought free will worked through the human ability to direct attention freely.[18] A present day humanistic psychologist, Viktor Frankl, sums up the existential freedom of attention by saying that the final human freedom, possible even when in a concentration camp where Frankl was incarcerated, is the ability to take up an attitude toward what is happening to one.[19] The freedom of evaluative attention can be had even when one is being coerced and events are out of personal control.

But, the ability to direct the attention of the I freely is not always an easy matter. The human organism is complicated, and even the self, or all that one can call one's own, is multidimensioned or multiple in nature. According to James, there is a material self, a multifaceted social self, and an intellectual self— all parts of the me that the innermost I can observe.[20] Achieving integration or unity can sometimes be difficult—as one aspect of the self may war against the innermost core self. (Indeed, in mental illness the "I" can lose all of its integrating force as serious disintegration, dissociation, and maladaption take place.) Altruistic decisions in which there is rebellion or resistance of a part of one's self can be difficult to achieve. The core self wills an action as most true to one's core self in the long run, but some other aspect of the self rebels and struggles for control. Christians have expressed this inner struggle as the flesh warring against the spirit.

The idea of a divided self needing integration and wholeness is certainly part of Christian tradition. Paul speaks of his inability to act as he would. One interpretation of Christ's saving act is that Jesus achieved full unity of spirit and nature as he gave his whole self in love. Christians have aspired to achieve this unity and integrity through Christ's indwelling Spirit. The search of the faithful for integration and transformation has always been metaphorically described as a kind of dying to the old self in order that the spirit or newly empowered self may be born and live.

The not yet transformed human self or I is burdened by inner divisions and the forces of inertia. But, I am also free enough as an agent to turn my attention to God's saving power. My attention can be fixed upon God in Christ who can transform me. As believers ask for help in faithful attentiveness to Love, power is received to enable us to love others as God loves us. When love abounds, we increase our works of mercy toward others. Faith is a work of attention which empowers works in the world. The effort of offering the mind, heart, and will to God in Christ, frees the Holy Spirit within to engender loving acts. Believers can act with, through, and in Christ to love and serve the world.

This transformative process of growing up into Christ our head is not easy, and it usually takes a lifetime's prolonged struggle. As noted above, the journey is different for each individual. And yet, the transformation should produce a certain family resemblance to Christ. There should be some likeness to Christ in those whom the Spirit has been transforming. When we talk of the gifts of the Holy Spirit, such as understanding and fortitude, and the fruits of the Holy Spirit, such as joy and peace, we are describing the qualities of transformed persons and their characteristic interactions with others. What emerges is a common psychological profile of a Christian personality which is uniquely expressed in a seemingly infinite variety of permutations. Great friends of God become more alike, while becoming ever more uniquely individual.

The central identifying characteristic of those growing up into Christ is merciful love towards others. So, the works of mercy will be the natural fruit of a Christian life. These actions of benevolence are the fruit of love and the way love is expressed and the way love grows ever more intense. I think a human being's relationship to God and to others and to the self is a three-way mutually interactive relationship. Movement can start in any pole and move to the others. Love of others, love of God, and love of self are intertwined.

But, is it the case that we can engender the emotion of love by a free personal act? I have already discussed the nature of emotions in regard to empathy, altruism, and love, but the question of whether emotions can be voluntary is a different problem. Much traditional wisdom, both secular and religious, has held that the emotions are passions suffered passively by the person. Emotions were thought to be part of our animal nature which came and went with our appetites and could hardly be initiated voluntarily. Control through suppression of all emotions might be possible, but not other kinds of active control. The Stoics advocated the ideal of *apatheia,* or a detachment from all desires, fears, or loves; the ideal was that no feeling should interfere with the pure governance of reason.

The old suspicion of emotions and fear of the overwhelming power of passion were founded on a false psychological model of human consciousness. Psychologists hold today that emotion is almost always a part of self consciousness; emotions intertwine with thought processes, and, in memory, emotions and thoughts may be stored together, triggering one another in recall processes.[21] It is also probably the case that emotions and concepts become fused and so can enter consciousness and memory as one cognitive-affective entity or structure. Emotions cannot be avoided in the stream of consciousness and permeate human thinking.

Indeed, emotions most often result from some instantaneous, preconscious, cognitive appraisals or rational reaction to the environment.[22] Emotions which seem to come out of the blue are instead signals from the self's memory of past experiences; they should be attended to as vital signs of inner and outer environments. When one considers the inevitability and rich resources of human emotions, it becomes clear that, instead of suppressing them, we should attempt to cultivate and educate emotions in ourselves and others.

Another mistake in older negative attitudes toward emotion was to notice and selectively look only at certain extreme, primitive, negative emotions as though this were the whole of emotional experience. It is true that extreme, infantile, regressed emotions of rage, lust, despair, and terror do seem to disrupt functioning, cause paralysis or violent, negative consequences. But, even these emotions come with some meaning or cognitive content (unless they are the result of brain damage or drugs). They, too, are signals of infantile, regressed reactions in a person — raw demands or terrors of infancy which have not been overcome.

What used to be interpreted as a conflict between heart and head, or emotion and thought, turns out to be more complex. The conflict within a person is usually between a primitive, childish, inappropriate cognitive-emotive scenario and interpretation of the world versus a more civilized, self-regulating, loving set of emotions and cognitive interpretations. It is not usually a case of conflict between pure emotion and pure reason, but of two different combinations of appraisals and emotions. Perhaps there is a childish, grandiose part-self which still exists in its untutored state.

But, primitive, childlike emotions fused with primitive interpretations of the world are hardly the whole story of human emotion. As we saw in the discussion of empathy and love, a large part of life is shaped by innately human, positive emotions, such as joy, love, and interest. These emotions early on can become blended, elaborated, and linked to certain interpretations of self and the world. The desire to be good and seek God's love is an emotion. The love of truth, justice, art, literature, and our interest in finding out what is real is an emotion. Positive emotions fuel thinking and intellectual quests. Our whole human life together in families and communities — and all of our civilization — is built upon our human abilities to feel bonds, desires, and loyalties that are far deeper than calculations of rational self interest. Emotions are now seen as the primary motivating system in human beings.

The challenge, then, for Christians and for a culture is to educate emotions in persons so that persons will have appropriate emotions and be motivated to act justly and with love for others. Heart and mind must be educated together to produce acts of benevolence to achieve a civilization of love. As mentioned above, the motivations for the works of mercy are a person's empathy, sympathy, and love toward those in need. And, yes, we want guilt and shame to be associated with harmful acts, selfish greed, and hardheartedness toward our neighbor. If we educate the whole person, mind and heart and will, we will produce persons who can intuitively discern what is appropriate when faced with new challenges and dilemmas in our common life.

In a sense, every human community and culture have always demanded that persons have certain emotions and control or suppress other harmful emotions. Moreover, if the proper emotions do not come spontaneously into consciousness, persons have been taught reeducational strategies to deal with their personal emotional inadequacies. They are told to think of beloved models or exercise other techniques of control. (Perhaps the most alarming modern development in our own society has been the discovery that certain persons can have such vast deficits in emotion that they cannot be reached by any remedial measures — the emotionless psychopath does not have intellectual deficits, but yet seems not to feel the necessary moral emotions of love, guilt, or shame.) But, within the normal range of functioning, our culture has held people accountable for educating and controlling their emotions and judged their character accordingly.[23] Whatever the given temperament or conditioning, we have expected unimpaired adults to shape a character in conformity with our cultural norms.

Christians in their communities have been commanded to love God and love their neighbor as they love themselves. The faithful are to love their families, communities, fellow members of the Church and, even more difficult, to love their enemies and those who injure them. Ironically, this demand for Christian love has often been made while intellectual beliefs about the negativity of emotion and an individual's inability to engender or control emotions have been the reigning ideology. Somehow the will was supposed to produce an agape or charitable love which was disconnected from emotional responses. In particularly problematic versions of this view of love and detachment, love of God was thought to be in direct competition with love of persons. Today, a more adequate approach to Christian love is developing which is less schizoid. Love of the unseen God and love of God in the neighbor we can see can hardly be in conflict.

But, my larger claim here is that emotions, at least positive emotions, can be freely engendered and that the positive emotion of merciful love and benevolence needed for the works of mercy can be induced by trying. I claim this ability only for the positive emotion of love and good will. Perhaps skilled method actors may be able to induce in themselves anger, sadness, and anxiety at will, but I am not sure whether a normal person, starting from a state of rest, can feel fear, hate, or contempt without a demagogue like Hitler or a personal Iago to play upon the person's insecurities and weaknesses. Yet, normal persons who have experienced a normal family environment without extreme abuse can engender benevolent love and mercy towards others. A Christian believer, in particular, should be able to fulfill the injunction to love others and perform the works of mercy. If this is so, how does one do it?

First, it helps to consider where spontaneous emotions, such as a feeling of love, come from. The spontaneous emotions that come into consciousness are usually the results of past choices and deployments of attention which have been encoded in memory. The long term memory system may filter the material coming into present consciousness and awareness, since everything in the internal and external environment could never be processed. What comes into consciousness is selected. A reaction that seems spontaneous is the result of what has been constructed or laid down in a person's memory in the past. For some people, the responses of love and mercy have been so often chosen and attended to that it has become habitual; like the heroic altruist, these persons instantaneously respond to others with love and to anyone in need with empathy, sympathy, and efforts to meet their need or rectify their deficit. But, when this loving reaction does not happen, a person can engender emotions in several ways. Thinking, imagining, feeling other emotions and actions can be used to engender emotions.

Since we know emotions are associated and often fused with thoughts and interpretations of certain thoughts, thinking of certain thoughts, images, and appraisals will produce the desired emotions associated with them in memory. Empathy and sympathy for another appear when a conviction of our shared humanity is brought to mind. Imaginatively taking the role of the other, identifying with the other's need produce sympathy.

Christians ask God directly to be empowered to love others, as we have discussed above. And, in the asking and praying, they think upon their faith in God as love and loving Creator of all. They bring to mind Christ's redemptive love of us and the Spirit's love in the world in which each person is one of God's beloved creations. The models of Christ and the saints are identified with so that we long to emulate those we love by loving as they loved. Certainly, Christians have traditionally used these and many other strategies of thought, imagination, and memory to induce love and acts of benevolence. One thinks here of the examples of the Ignatian exercises which have empowered so many to serve others.

Emotions are also shaped by other emotions. A feeling of love can overcome a spontaneous feeling of disgust at the condition of others — be they ill, poor, dirty or, in a more subtle problem, sinful, cruel, vapid, or stupid. Anger or moral indignation can transform helplessness before injustice into willed action for reforms — as the Hebrew prophets understood. Sadness can defuse anger. Love and trust in God cast out fear. Gratitude overcomes envy. Joy and interest blend to create love. Moments of joy tutor us in love. If I feel pity, I can hardly feel vengeance and hate. So, the effort here is again to feel as Christ would feel — or, through prayerful love, to live and feel as the new transformed and redeemed self.

Another way that emotions are engendered and shaped is through behavioral acts. We recognize that physical acts can defuse and dissipate emotional states of stress, fear, anger, and despair. We exercise and work and feel differently. Action produces hope and perseverance. Other behavioral strategies of a more meditative kind also engender different emotional states. Those adept at meditation have used breathing, postures, and other physical means to control anxiety and fear, and thereby create a calm readiness to feel in certain positive ways.

Behavior and overt action influence thought and feeling as well as the other way round. One sure way for love and benevolence to be engendered is through acts of love and mercy. To do acts of benevolence engenders the emotion of love. As one comforts or counsels or feeds or clothes or acts on behalf of another's good, the associated feelings of empathy, care, and sympathy arise from the engaged encounter. In the same way, torturing and aggressively hurting others produce hatred for them; just turning a deaf ear to pain and suffering hardens the heart for next time. Physically and psychologically caring for another produces emotional caring. Our attention is engaged, and our will to love increases.

These many strategies for an individual to engender benevolent love depend upon the teaching and modeling of a community. As social creatures dependent upon culture, humans would find it almost impossible to counter the influences of an uncaring, hostile culture or hatefilled group without community support. Human individuals learn through interaction with others. To learn to engender positive emotions that produce benevolent acts, an individual needs to live within a community, beginning, if possible, with the family, which is displaying models of love in attitude and deed — and teaching the young to act in an altruistic manner. The Good News must be experienced first hand, although a person may be innately prepared to hear it through our common human nature. In Christian communities, the works of mercy have to be taught and exemplified before individual members can learn the way to love one another as God has loved us. How might we encourage and nurture the works of mercy?

How can we encourage the works of mercy?

One of the most important conditions for performing works of mercy is affirming the interpersonal context in which we live. Since the focus and object of a loving act are to meet the need of another person who is also an acting subject, these actions are always person-to-person, never person-to-thing, enterprises. The interpersonal context of almost all of the works of mercy means that there is always reciprocity in a living relationship. The spiritual works of mercy in particular preclude any distancing of self from the person in need. The need can be met only in a personal relationship by a voluntary psychological response on the part of the person being helped. The help being given

precludes a Lady Bountiful who hands out baskets of fruit inter-
changeably to one and all and then departs the scene.

Loving benevolence pays attention to the individual person
as a unique person, made in the image of God, and as a temple
of the Spirit of God. The human dignity of the other must be
acknowledged, along with the psychological and social uniqueness of each person. We know that the self is many dimensioned
and that the inner self of selves is fused with bodily self, social
selves, and cognitive, linguistic, cultural selves. All of these dimensions of the person need to be respected in another—as well
as in ourselves.

Early in our lives, as infant studies seem to show, we develop
an intersubjective, interpersonal social self which can operate
along with linguistic interchanges.[24] The self is formed by life
with others so we are ready to enter into emotional intersubjective communication with others, along with language communication. Human beings are not individualistic monads, drifting
around in separated orbits until we can give informed consent
to contractual alliances. We possess private inner centers of
consciousness, but we are also embedded in interpersonal relationships and networks of community from the beginning of life
to the end. This embeddedness that exists along with shared
language means that it is possible to reach another in an intersubjective understanding deeper than words. Heart can speak
to heart. Communication is more than speech, since emotions
and actions also convey meaning.

The works of mercy are whole actions of whole persons and
may be done with words, shared emotions, and shared actions.
Our speech, actions, and emotions will be part of our message
to others. We read each other's emotions in face, posture, voice,
and other subtle cues. If loving benevolence is being conveyed,
it is conveyed on all levels. How demeaning it is to be the object
of help given begrudgingly or scornfully! How far from the love
and respect that characterize God's mercy! We are told to perform acts for others as we would for Christ. Physically, emotionally, and linguistically we try to express love as we try to meet
the need of another.

The reciprocity of all helping relationships is also important.
If, as a Christian, we believe in the equality of all children of
God, we can be open to learn and receive from everyone we
meet. We must listen; we must, above all, pay attention to this
person and this particular, specific set of circumstances here
and now impinging upon this life or this community. In efforts
to help people with physical needs, the most loving action will
be to try to serve their longterm interests as well as their short-

term need. Help which will enable others to feed, clothe, and shelter themselves will be the most valuable. Those whose works of mercy focus on righting injustice and changing unjust structures of poverty will work to give the most effective help in the long run. Justice means giving others equal opportunities and equalizing power among all.

In the spiritual works of mercy with individuals, it takes a great deal of careful attention before one can even know what will help another. To instruct, or to counsel, even to comfort another requires entering into his/her reality and meeting him/her where he/she is now. The self-emptying of the Godhead in love becomes a very practical model for being with another who needs help. The person who desires to help another psychologically or spiritually must be humble and listen. Yet, we may be more prepared for performing the spiritual works of mercy than we are for performing others. Few affluent persons have ever been hungry or homeless or imprisoned, but everyone has suffered in mind and heart. Everyone has been ignorant or misguided. The person trying to help another psychologically and spiritually has experiences in common which make empathy and mutuality easier. Such encounters can always be a two-way relationship of giving and getting.

A concept of the wounded healer has been used to describe the way that those who have suffered, particularly suffered in the same way as the person now in need, are better prepared to be helpers. Peer counseling and fellow sufferers help explain the success of Alcoholics Anonymous and other self help groups. But, it is better that the person who is offering help should not at the time still be in the throes of his/her own suffering. His/her wounds should be healed enough so that he/she has strength to help another, rather than adding to the distress and helplessness of the encounter.

There are also those spiritual works of mercy which are not only psychologically difficult to perform, but are directly countercultural to the norms of our society. Modern Americans approve of physically helping others, and they believe in comforting others, counseling others, and instructing others. But, to admonish those who are sinning or positively address those who wrong and injure others is another matter. One tenet of the modern creed is to mind one's own business when it comes to moral, ethical, and religious questions.

In these uncomfortable cases, the persons we must love and help are not naturally appealing in their need; they often put us off by their failings or harmful actions. They are offensive because they are engaging in sinful, wrong, or injurious acts which are hurting others and us personally. Wrongdoers resist being admonished, hate having their wrongs exposed, and do not desire to be forgiven since that means admitting they have injured others. Here, the Christian faces the greatest crisis and challenge of faith because the model and words of Christ and our tradition are at odds with the wisdom of the world and our natural inclinations. From the modern secular point of view, only praying for another who is either living or already dead can seem more useless than bearing wrongs patiently. While each of these most difficult works of mercy can be examined and explored in great depth, I will look at only one countercultural command more closely: to admonish the sinner.

Who wishes to admonish the sinner in a world in which freedom of choice, privacy, and autonomy are accepted as the ultimate cultural dogmas? In addition, much of secular society's reluctance to become involved in another person's moral and religious practice comes from an underlying acceptance of cultural relativism. Considering the array of moral beliefs and practices found everywhere, who can tell what is right or wrong for another person? Indeed, a belief in the existence of sin or moral evil is suspect. To admonish the sinner, one has to believe that a person freely chooses to do something seriously wrong when he or she knows better. The doubts about the human ability to freely sin arise from the lingering determinism in the culture which makes us unsure that persons are free enough to overcome their environmental conditioning or their innate genetic programming. Can they really help it when they commit an offense? It is easier to give everyone the benefit of the doubt and not get involved.

But, if I am my brother's or sister's keeper, I can not rest easy with a detached attitude toward others. Such a skeptical stance is also untrue to the Christian conviction that we are free to choose and can be responsible for ourselves and others as well. It is fairly easy to believe in sin when I know that I am a sinner — and I can hardly be alone. Most ordinary people may not ever enact a mortal sin in which a free, clear, final repudiation of God is made involving a serious matter. But, other sins exist. Unfortunately, we can perhaps most know and see the sins of those close to us — the very persons whose failures hurt us most, and we them. If we do not speak, are we not colluding or enabling a person's wrong actions?

Inertia, laziness, hatred of conflict always counsel avoidance of any trouble; any cost-benefit calculus usually demonstrates that a high price may have to be paid for any confrontation. But, love cares about the ultimate longterm good of another person. There is also a concern for the harm that a person who sins may be doing to others as well as to self. Love leads us to speak.

It is well to remember here that admonishing another is not the same as condemning, attacking, or nagging in order to dominate another person. Admonishing a sinner means gently and kindly reproving or reminding a person of a serious matter involving his/her own violation of his/her own moral standards. It is exhorting, warning, or confronting someone with what he/she already knows is wrong. (If he/she truly did not know something was wrong, then you might be called to instruct the ignorant, but not confront a sinner.) In sinning, a person knows and chooses to act in a seriously wrong way. The hope of the one admonishing is that the loving witness of the admonition will help the person to turn again and live. It may, however, fail. Jesus himself was not (and many a great saint since has not been) successful in every effort to confront another. People are truly free to refuse or accept the good.

There are many ways to admonish another, and many different circumstances in which it is appropriate if one loves or cares for another. Since one wishes to be heard and get the message across successfully, it is a case of trying to be as shrewd as a serpent and as innocent as a dove. A Christian must also practice self examination first to avoid the mote-beam problem and make sure that one's life will not prove one a hypocrite to be discounted. If a person is going to admonish others, there must be a readiness to be admonished. Only others can tell you things that efforts at self deception may have avoided seeing.

To breach personal defenses is always a painful thing. Obviously, there can be different costs and outcomes to admonishing, depending upon the differentials of power between persons and whether it is a private or more public act. Admonishing can become a public, political act when used by someone like Gandhi or Martin Luther King. But, for most of us the action will be taken in private life with those we know well.

The closer in affection, the more common ideals we share, the more imperative the need to admonish one another. The more in common shared with another, the more clear it can be that another is falling into sin. God, Jesus, and the saints always seem more critical of their own followers who should know better. Christians have received more and, therefore, have more expected of them. The faithful have always admonished each other, sometimes calling it evangelical criticism and seeing it as vital to building up the community.[25] Paul constantly admonished his beloved church communities and told them: "In wis-

dom made perfect, instruct and admonish one another"
(Colossians 3:16).

One can go about giving another an unpleasant message in
many ways—through a symbolic action, gesture, or look, or
story, or through direct verbal communication given at a critical
or propitious moment. One thinks of the look Jesus gave Peter
after the betrayal, or some of the stories Jesus told in response
to his quarreling disciples. In the incident of the woman taken
in adultery, Jesus admonished the accusers by setting the impossible condition as the permission to throw the first stone; he
admonished the woman herself with simple, loving words: "Go
and sin no more." If we love each other, we must help each other
by admonishing one another with courage.

Here, we come back once more to the critical relationship
between the individual and the community. Underlying the
whole idea of meeting the needs and deficits of others is the
belief that we are interdependent and united in communion,
while also unique, free individuals. Human beings are viewed
as united, fallen together in Adam, and redeemed together in
Christ. Living as one, as a human family with Christ as an elder
brother or firstborn, human beings must take care of one another. The physical, social, moral, and religious wellbeing of
one affects all those united in Christ. We are members of one
another.

The moral and spiritual concern for others is appropriate if
we are, in truth, members of one body and one family. Our
common nature as equally beloved children of God, all made in
God's image, motivates benevolence and makes love effective.
Since we are alike in sharing human nature, we can have empathy and understanding enough to know what others need and
give it to them. When we open ourselves to Christ's love for us
and in us, we can love others. Their welfare and our welfare are
intimately entwined.

In a more mysterious way, we sense that what we do and the
way we do it have import for all. As we strive to relieve suffering, to help others grow, to grow and be faithful ourselves, there
comes the realization that not only are all the hairs on our head
numbered, but our deeds and thoughts matter for us and everyone else. The "little way" of doing everything large and small for
God seems to have meaning beyond the moment. Our work
and our suffering are somehow used for everyone; nothing is
lost, no matter how obscure and hidden. Testimony to this truth
comes from great mystics and spiritual persons. Natan
Sharansky, a prisoner of conscience who refused to give in to the

KGB, expressed this feeling when, in his lonely cell, he concluded:

> I formulated for myself a new law: the law of universal attraction, interconnection, and interdependence of human souls....In addition to Newton's law of the universal gravitational pull of objects, there is also a universal gravitational pull of souls, of the bond between them and the influence of one soul on the other. With each word we speak and each step we take, we touch other souls and have an impact on them.[26]

In conclusion, we can see that the traditional works of mercy, enjoined on all Christians, testify to the unity of the human family. The Church's call to perform these works remains a witness to the belief that love in action is possible.

NOTES

[1]See Sidney Callahan, *With All Our Heart & Mind: The Spiritual Works of Mercy in a Psychological Age* (New York: Crossroad, 1990). In research for this book, I could find little research or analysis.

[2]John Paul II, *Laborem Exercens (Encyclical On Human Work)* (Boston: Daughters of St. Paul, 1981), 5: "Work is one of the characteristics that distinguish man from the rest of creatures, whose activity for sustaining their lives cannot be called work."

[3]There is a huge literature on consciousness. See in particular Kenneth S. Pope and Jerome L. Singer, "The Waking Stream of Consciousness," in *The Psychobiology of Consciousness,* ed. Julian M. Davidson and Richard J. Davidson (New York: Plenum Press, 1980), 169-91.

[4]William James, "The Consciousness of Self," in *The Principles of Psychology,* Vol. 1 (New York: Dover Publications, 1950 [1890]), 291-401.

[5]See John F. Kihlstrom, "Conscious, Subconscious, Unconscious: A Cognitive Perspective," in *The Unconscious Reconsidered,* ed. Kenneth S. Bowers and Donald Meichenbaum (New York: John Wiley & Sons, 1984), 149-211.

[6]A confident assertion about God and the unconscious can be found in the popular work of M. Scott Peck who asserts, "What this suggests is that the interface between God and man is at least in part the interface between our unconscious and our conscious. To put it plainly, our unconscious is God. God within us." M. Scott Peck, *The Road Less Travelled* (New York: Simon and Schuster, 1978), 281.

[7]Karl Rahner, "Perseverance," in *The Practice of Faith: A Handbook of Contemporary Spirituality* (New York: Crossroad, 1986), 267.

[8]See Mihaly Csikszentmihalyi, "The Merging of Action and Awareness," in *Flow: The Psychology of Optimal Experience* (New York: Harper & Row, 1990), 53-54.

[9]There has been a recent explosion in psychological research on human emotion. I follow most closely the theory of human emotion set

forth by Carroll E. Izard, in his classic formulation, *Human Emotions* (New York: Plenum Press, 1977).

[10]See, for instance, Joseph J. Campos and Karen Caplovitz Barrett, "Toward a new understanding of emotions and their development," in *Emotions, Cognition and Behavior,* ed. Carroll E. Izard, Jerome Kagan, and Robert B. Zajonc (Cambridge: Cambridge Univ. Press, 1984), 229-63.

[11]A prototypical example of a recent discussion of the importance of cognition in emotion can be found in Richard S. Lazarus, "Cognition and Motivation in Emotion," *American Psychologist* 46 (April, 1991): 352-67.

[12]Martin L. Hoffman, "Empathy, Its Limitations, and Its Role in a Comprehensive Moral Theory," in *Morality, Moral Behavior, and Moral Development,* ed. William M. Kurtines and Jacob L. Gewirtz (New York: John Wiley & Sons, 1984), 283-302.

[13]Martin L. Hoffman discusses "existential guilt" in "Empathy, Role Taking, Guilt and Development of Altruistic Motives," in *Moral Development and Behavior: Theory, Research and Social Issues,* ed. Thomas Lickona (New York: Holt, Rinehart and Winston, 1976), 124-43; for a philosophical discussion of nonmoral guilt, see Herbert Morris, "Nonmoral guilt," in *Responsibility, Character, and the Emotions: New Essays in Moral Psychology,* ed. Ferdinand Schoeman (Cambridge: Cambridge University Press, 1987), 220-40.

[14]George James, "Notes Tell of Painful Search by Jews Hidden during War," *The New York Times,* 27 May 1991, 24.

[15]Abraham H. Maslow, "Notes on Synergy," *Eupsychian Management: A Journal* (Homewood, Illinois: The Dorsey Press, 1965), 88.

[16]Albert Bandura, "Self-efficacy mechanism in human Agency," *American Psychologist* 37 (1982): 122-47.

[17]See Karl H. Pribram, "The Cognitive Revolution and Mind/ Brain Issues," *American Psychologist* 41 (May, 1986): 507-20; see also R. W. Sperry, "Psychology's Mentalist Paradigm and the Religion Science Tension," *American Psychologist* 43 (August, 1988): 607-13.

[18]James, *op.cit.,* 258; see also a modern psychological analysis of the self-regulation of consciousness in Csikszentmihalyi, *op.cit.,* 71-93; for a philosophical analysis of the way freedom of attention relates to freedom of the will, see Harry G. Frankfurt, "Freedom of the Will and the Concept of a Person," in *What Is a Person?,* ed. Michael F. Goodman (Clifton, NJ: Humana Press, 1988), 127-44.

[19]Viktor E. Frankl, *Man's Search For Meaning* (New York: Washington Square Press, 1984 [1946]).

[20]James, *op.cit.,* 291-401; see also Gordon Allport, *Becoming* (New Haven: Yale University Press, 1955).

[21]Gordon H. Bower and Paul R. Cohen, "Emotional Influences in Memory and Thinking: Data and Theory," in *Affect and Cognition: The Seventeenth Annual Carnegie Symposium on Cognition,* ed. Margaret Sydnor Clark and Susan T. Fiske (Hillsdale, NJ: Lawrence Erlbaum, 1982), 291-332.

[22]Richard S. Lazarus, *op.cit.*

[23]John Sabini and Maury Silver, "Emotions, responsibility, and character," in *Responsibility, Character and the Emotions,* 165-75.

[24]Daniel N. Stern, "Affect Attunement," in *The Interpersonal World of the Infant: A View from Psychoanalysis and Developmental Psychology* (New York: Basic Books, 1985), 138-61.

[25]José I. Gonzalez Faus, *Where the Spirit Breathes: Prophetic Dissent in the Church* (Maryknoll, New York: Orbis, 1989).

[26]Natan Sharansky, *Fear No Evil* (New York: Random House, 1988), 362.

The Works of Mercy: Theological Perspectives

Francis Schüssler Fiorenza

I. A CHALLENGE

In a recent essay, the African-American theologian, James Cone, quoted from a leaflet distributed at a poor people's rally in Albuquerque, New Mexico, entitled, "Listen Christians":

Listen Christians,
I was hungry
and you formed a humanities club
and you discussed my hunger
Thank you.

I was imprisoned
and you crept off quietly
to your chapel in the cellar
and prayed for my release.

I was naked
and in your mind
you debated the morality of
my appearances

I was sick
and you knelt and thanked God
for your health

I was homeless
and you preached to me
of the spiritual shelter of
the love of God

I was lonely

31

and you left me alone
to pray for me
You seem so holy;
so close to God.

But I'm still very hungry
and lonely
and cold
So where have your prayers
gone?
What have they done?

What does it profit a man
to page through his book of prayers
when the rest of the world
is crying for his help?

These words confront us as well-to-do believers. They challenge us, as James Cone has poignantly asked: "How can one
speak about the church of the body of the crucified Jesus of
Nazareth when church people are so healthy and well fed and
have no broken bones?"[1] These words remind us that the works
of mercy determine who we are as Christians and the way we as
Christians should live.

A. THE CHALLENGE OF THE SCRIPTURES

The Parable of the Last Judgment challenges us as Christians, when it makes the works of mercy the criterion of Christian existence and Christian salvation. Whether the Son of Man
at the final judgment acknowledges one as his own depends
upon whether one has fed the hungry, given drink to the thirsty,
welcomed the stranger, clothed the naked, and visited the sick
and those in prison. Persons who claim to be righteous because
of their pious deeds, but who have not done the works of mercy,
will not be acknowledged by the Son of Man, but will be subject
to eternal punishment. This parable equates works of mercy
toward the needy with works of mercy toward Jesus himself. In
the view of some scholars, this parable displays elements of
Matthean redaction, and yet probably goes back to Jesus himself (Matthew 25:31-46).[2] It has its antecedents both in apoca-
lyptic Jewish traditions and in Judaic traditions that connect the
works of love and the Torah. Yet, its radical equation between
the love of God and the love of the least of the brethren emphasizes a relation that has become central to Christian identity
and self understanding.
The Epistle of James poses a similar challenge: "If a brother
or a sister is ill-clad and in lack of daily food, and one of you

says to them, 'Go in peace, be warmed and filled,' without giving them the things needed for the body, what does it profit?' So
faith by itself, if it has no works, is dead" (James 2:14-17). These
verses, which stress the care for the poor, belong, as Martin
Dibelius has argued, to prophetic traditions within the earliest
strata of the New Testament. They "express an ethos typical of
early Christianity."[3]

These challenges are clear; yet, a certain ambiguity exists today about the works of mercy. The very term, "works of mercy,"
is no longer in vogue, which, in turn, raises the question: why
does one less commonly refer to the "works of mercy"? Moreover, many complain that the churches today have become too
involved in social work and too concerned with political liberation so that they have neglected their truly religious task.[4] Liberation and political theologies also seem to shy away from
speaking about the works of mercy insofar as such discourse
would express an individual, rather than a structural and political, approach to social ills. These critical reservations and questions urge that one reflect on the meaning of the biblical
challenge today. What does it mean for us that the hungry, the
poor, the sick, the homeless, and the imprisoned represent
Christ? How should the works of mercy constitute the criteria
for Christian salvation? What does it mean that the works of
mercy are not secondary beliefs and practices of Christian communities, but, instead, constitute their identity? Such questions
should be addressed within the context of issues which political
or liberation theology raises concerning the significance of social structures and political organizations for the amelioration
of social needs.[5]

B. THEOLOGICAL REFLECTION: A COMPLEX PERSPECTIVE

This essay addresses the works of mercy from a theological
perspective. Theological reflection is often understood in various ways. For some, theology is a set of doctrines, teachings,
convictions that one ascertains and then applies to particular
problems. For others, theological reflection consists of drawing
a set of convictions and beliefs primarily from the Bible and
then applying them to a current issue or situation. A business
school once asked me to talk on the theology of work. The
school had prepared a poster for the talk that depicted the Bible
on one side and a hammer and anvil on the other. Obviously,
the business school understood theology as the application of
biblical teachings to the problem of work. Similarly, many,

though with more nuance, view theology as a correlation between biblical symbols or between a tradition's religious symbols and concrete existential questions today.

Theology, however, is indeed a much more complex endeavor. Four elements are integral to a comprehensive theological method, and each is essential to the theological task.[6] The *first* is what I would call the interpretation of the tradition or, more specifically, the interpretation of what makes up the integrity of the religious tradition. This interpretation includes not just the Bible, not just some theologians, nor even individual magisterial statements, but the tradition in its integrity and with its broad spectrum of affirmations. Attempts at such an interpretation encounter a diversity of practices, different priorities, and even conflicts within the tradition. The interpretation must then discriminate. It must ask what is paradigmatic, what is more central, what is overriding, what forms the integrity of the tradition? This first task of interpretation or, to use a technical term, of a hermeneutical reconstruction, however, should be done, not in isolation, but only in combination with the other elements of a theological method.[7]

The *second* element involves *background* theories, assumptions, and structures. In examining a religious tradition, one considers relevant background theories and examines such background assumptions that are implicit and operative within the tradition, influencing, and even determining, the judgments of the tradition. For example, in the case of the theological works of mercy, one can and should ask: What understanding of society was implied in various historical periods of the tradition, or what significance do societal changes have for the affirmations of the tradition? Do these societal changes require that theological reflection radically rethink the significance and practice of the works of mercy? Or, do the values affirmed in the tradition still have meaning, but within a changed societal and political context? Or, is the alternative itself false, and is it the task of theological reflection to demonstrate that?

The *third* element involves the community's ongoing experience and practice. Theological reflection considers warrants that stem from present experience and from ongoing practice. Practice or praxis, as it is more comprehensively called, does not entail simply the application of knowledge and insight to concrete situations. Instead, practice is a source of knowledge and learning. Theology often moves retrospectively or retroductively from experience back to a new, deeper, and often changed understanding of its theories and tradition. The committed practice of a community constitutes an experience and a source of knowledge from which it interprets its past tradition and present viewpoints.

Fourth, a theological perspective on the works of mercy needs the insights of community as a community of discourse and interpretation. The voices of the poor within our country—as expressed in the quoted pamphlet—as well as the voices of the impoverished people in other parts of the globe belong to the community of humankind. They are voices to whom we must listen.

In approaching this theological task, I shall first briefly survey the historical praxis of the works of mercy throughout the Christian tradition, noting its constants and its changes. Then, I shall examine two interpretations of the works of mercy: Thomas Aquinas's analysis of the works of mercy and a sixteenth century theological debate about the prohibition of begging in some cities. Thomas Aquinas represents the medieval interpretation that has become paradigmatic in the tradition. The debate during the Renaissance highlights significant issues in the transition to modern society. Next, a discussion of background assumptions concerning the structures of society and of societal changes will provide the horizon for examining the role of the works of mercy within contemporary society. Finally, I shall argue that, though the works of mercy are still an essential criterion of Christian identity, the changed conditions of modern society have deeply affected their praxis. The existence of social welfare policy requires changes in the critical and practical roles of Christian communities.

II. WORKS OF MERCY: HISTORICAL PRAXIS

I begin my theological perspective on the works of mercy by briefly alluding to salient examples of the works of mercy within the history of Christianity: early, medieval, and modern. This brief sketch of the praxis of the works of mercy aims to sketch some constants and changes, some points of identity and transformation, that can provide warrants for a constructive interpretation of Christian identity in regard to the theological interpretation of the works of mercy.

A. EARLY CHRISTIANITY

In early Christianity, the works of mercy were integral to the Christian community. Since the Christian Scriptures make the works of mercy the criterion of salvation, as in the Parable of the Final Judgment, then the praxis of the early Christian communities, both in New Testament times and the centuries immediately following, shows the struggle to take this challenge seriously. The communities develop forms of life-praxis as well as liturgical praxis that constitute a community in which charity and mercy are integral to its religious, as well as ethical, life.

As these communities developed in the early centuries, the works of mercy became organized and centered in the office of the Presider at the Eucharist or the Bishop.[8] Regular collections, both of money and of goods, large donations, and sporadic collections for specific needs or occasions were all made. Money was often collected and held in what could be called the community's "bank." These were called the "gazophylaciuon Dei"[9] of orphans and widows, sick and needy, prisoners and strangers. A link often existed between the sick and needy because those sick often became needy to the extent that their illness made it impossible to work and obtain the essentials of life.

Justin, in his *First Apology,* described that, at the conclusion of the Sunday service after the Eucharistic prayer, the members of the community bring gifts forward to the presider and these gifts are, in turn, distributed among the poor and needy:

> Those who are wealthy and others who wish each offer a donation according to their choice, and what is collected is brought to the presiding officer, and with this he assists orphans, widows, and those who are in need through illness or any other reason; also those who are in prison, strangers from other lands, and in short, he takes care of all those who may be in want.[10]

As this form of almsgiving became increasingly institutionalized, the office of deacon increasingly had the task of determining who was really in need. The care of the sick was centered in the local church community. A varied development took place. At first, the works of mercy were administered at the parochial level insofar as they were primarily performed by the local community. Later, the diocese became the center of their administration, and then, later on, the works of mercy were decentralized from the diocese back to the parish.

The theological justification of the works of mercy, especially almsgiving, is exemplified by St. Cyprian's treatise, "On Works and Alms" (ca. 254). Cyprian appealed to the Scriptures for prototypes illustrating the nature and value of almsgiving, such as, the widow who gave food to Elias, not out of abundance, but from very little that she and her children had (3 Kings 17). Likewise, Tobit advised his son to give alms from his possessions even if little (Tobit 4, 5-11). Moreover, Daniel's advice to King Nebuchadnezzar, that alms deliver from sin and death (Dan 4, 27), anticipates what becomes concrete in the narrative of Peter's resurrection of Tabitha from death on account of her good works and almsgiving (Acts 9, 50).[11]

In describing the significance of the works of mercy, Cyprian provided an ecclesial, Christological, and theological justification. The charity manifest in the works of mercy expresses the Christian community's unity of love. This charity is exemplified in God's gift of his Son and Christ's gift of his life for us. A further theological foundation for the works of mercy lies in the view of God's creation as belonging to God and the social implications drawn from this view: "For whatsoever is of God, is in our using common, nor is any human person shut out from God's bounties and gifts, to the end the whole human race may equally enjoy God's goodness and bounty."[12] Just as the light shines on all equally, so, too, does the person who shares his or her good imitate God. This theological justification locates the works of mercy, not simply as a matter of beneficence, but as a matter of justice.

This theological justification often came to be invoked in regard to the property and goods of the Church. "The goods of the church are the goods of the poor" was an expression that appeared in many local councils and synods toward the end of the early Christian period (For example, Clermont 535, Orleans 538 and 541, Paris 614). During the Pontificate of Simplicius (468-483) and Gelasius (492-496), it was decreed that one fourth of all the goods of the Church should be given to the poor.

B. MEDIEVAL CHRISTIANITY

The medieval period continued many practices of early Christianity. Yet, several distinctive developments took place.[13] One was the segmentation, institutionalization, and specialization of the works of mercy. With all due caution, lest "institutionalization" be understood anachronistically, such a tendency is present in the practice of personal and social assistance.[14] This can be seen in the development of the medieval hospital (a much more diverse institution than the contemporary hospital), the role of the monasteries in the care of the poor and sick, the emergence of specific religious orders committed to the works of mercy, and the increasing role of the medieval city in the care of the needy — a development marking a transition point from the medieval to the early modern period.[15]

Hospitals: The early hospital should not be simply equated with our modern hospital.[16] Often called "Houses of God," they provided hospitality and shelter not only for the ill, but also for the poor, pilgrims, and travelers. At first, hospitals were often wings of monasteries. Later, hospitals became independent, and they were supported by the cities. During the medieval period, hospitals became specialized and diversified. In the fifteenth century, the author of the first distinct treatise on the works of mercy, Anthony of Fiorenza (the medieval spelling of the name of the city of Florence), distinguished among the *syndochium* — which gave lodging to the poor and pilgrims, the *procotrophium* — which gave food, the *gerontocomium* — which was open to the elderly, the *orphanotropium,* the orphanage, and the *brephotropium* — which was established to nourish infants. Though Anthony did not mention it, recent historical studies show that the majority of the poor who received help were women and children. The feminization of poverty, that is so obvious today, was present within the medieval period.

Monasteries and Religious Orders: Further developments are the increased role of the monasteries in taking care of the poor and sick and the transformation of the understanding of poverty associated with mendicant religious orders. During this period, the lands and wealth of the monasteries increased. The tithe given to the feudal lord went to the monasteries. The result enabled the monasteries to provide for the needy.[17] Recently, some social historians have questioned whether this help had geographic limitations in terms of access to the monasteries. The development of new orders led to some specialization. For example, Orders like the Trinitarians were established for the sake of ransoming captives of the Crusades. Other orders were concerned with the care of the sick. Very significant, however, was the rise of the mendicant religious orders which, with their voluntary poverty, brought to consciousness the existence of much involuntary poverty.

Cities and Church: The care of the poor within the cities was a concern of the churches. When the cities themselves took measures in regard to the poor and needy, the bishops were often enjoined by local synods to exercise oversight over this assistance. Just as the bishops criticized the Roman Empire in regard to social matters, so, too, was there their social criticism of cities concerning the adequacy of their care. Several of the councils recommend that the bishops watch out for the care of the poor.

Despite the development of these institutions and practices, the medieval period has often been criticized. Some criticisms have been directed against the understanding of the works of mercy as expressions of charity. Other criticisms have challenged the efficacy of the works of mercy. Focusing on social history and on new means of collecting and analyzing data,

some recent historical French scholarship has further illumi-
nated the issues of poverty and social assistance.[18] Its assessment
of the medieval period has been more nuanced than were early,
more critical treatments. On the one hand, this research has
pointed out that, even though certain economic developments
within the medieval period led to increased poverty and need in
the countryside, the "pauperization" that has emerged in modern industrial society did not exist in the medieval period. On
the other hand, one has argued that the medieval forms of social
assistance did not suffice. For example, the assistance of the
monastery was *de facto* limited to those living within a dozen or
so miles from the monasteries because of limited means of
transportation.[19]

C. CHRISTIAN PRAXIS WITHIN MODERNITY

Significant changes in the practice of the works of mercy take
place during modernity. These changes began in the Renaissance period, characterized not only by significant intellectual
changes, but also by social changes in the economic order as a
result of market economies. The intellectual changes became
fully evident in the Enlightenment. It is the political as well as
intellectual revolutions of the Enlightenment that led to the profound social and economic changes that constitute modernity. It
is these changes that significantly affected the practice of the
works of mercy.

In Europe, many Church properties were secularized in that
State and Civil authorities took over buildings belonging to
churches and land belonging to monasteries. Consequently,
monasteries and religious orders could not exercise the care of
the poor in the same way they had in the medieval period.
Alongside the process of secularization, changes in the economic and social order moved European society increasingly
away from a more agrarian to a more mercantile and industrial
society.

The Enlightenment was also an intellectual revolution, both
religious and philosophic. Criticism arose concerning many beliefs and practices of institutional religion, including the practices of almsgiving and the works of mercy. These criticisms,
though having their antecedents in the Renaissance debates,
became much more radical during the Enlightenment. Almsgiving was now thought to encourage laziness. The churches
were, therefore, responsible for poverty and laziness of beggars.
Instead of almsgiving, the need for a preventive and systemic
social approach to poverty was advocated. Consequently, the

role of the State continued to change, and there was an increased interest in social politics and in more structurally organized social assistance.

The effects of such measures have led to several significant
developments in the churches themselves. Three of these developments are: the concern for specific types of help within
churches inspired by Pietism, the development of new religious
orders and lay groups within Catholicism, and the increasing
concern in the churches with social policy, first in relation to the
development of the modern industrial West, with capitalist and
socialist economic systems, and then to the growing discrepancy between the developed countries and the less developed
countries.

Pietism and Alternative Models: As the industrialization of the
West took place, the traditional means of caring for the poor
within an agrarian economy collapsed. The churches had a significant role in developing new forms of social care, and these
new forms were, in turn, eventually taken over by the State. In
emphasizing a community of love and piety, Pietism sought to
care for the ill, for the poor, and for those imprisoned. Pietism
developed communal forms of social care that foreshadowed
many modern social services and organizations of welfare.[20]

New Religious Orders and Lay Groups: If the Medieval Church
gave rise to religious orders, a similar development takes place
within modernity. Specific religious orders emerge to deal with
the specific works of mercy: Daughters of Charity, Sisters of
Mercy, Salesians, Vincentians. Sometimes in the case of
women, however, the original intentions of the founder were
frustrated due to the Roman views of the role of women. For
example, the Visitation Order was established, as its name indicates, to have sisters visit persons in hospitals and in their
homes, but it was turned into a contemplative community. In
addition, lay institutes and organizations were established to
deal with charity; best known today are still the St. Vincent de
Paul Society and the Catholic Worker Group. In seventeenth-
century France and Italy, religious lay organization played an
increasing role in regard to the works of mercy. One could characterize this process as the "secularization" of the works of
mercy, not only insofar as the State took over forms of mercy
previously done by the churches, but also insofar as, within
Protestantism as well as Catholicism, lay people began to institute charitable programs through the formation of guilds, confraternities, and quasi-religious orders.[21]

Church as Social Critic: During the last hundred years, papal
encyclicals, from Leo XIII's *Rerum Novarum* to John Paul II's

Centesimus Annus, have critically examined poverty, exploitation, the negative effects of modern economic life. Socialism as well as capitalism, a market economy as well as a completely planned economy, have come under scrutiny in terms of their effects upon human dignity and human nature. Within the last two decades, both political theology and liberation theology have developed as significant theological movements that the mission of the Church include a critique of political ideologies and oppressive social structures.[22]

D. CONSTANTS AND TRANSFORMATIONS

This brief survey indicates significant constants as well as important transformations in the praxis of the works of mercy throughout the history of Christianity. Three constants are centrality, communality, and societal critique.

1. Three Constants

Centrality: the works of mercy were central to Christian religious life and praxis. This centrality to religious life in Christian praxis belies dualistic conceptions that split the religious and social life. Such conceptions view the religious and spiritual life on one level and the works of mercy at another, more material, level. Instead, the works of mercy were central to the religious life of the Church throughout its history. In the early Church, they were an integral part of the liturgy. Their practice was viewed as central to the tasks of bishops, clergy, deacons, and Christians. In the Medieval Church, the works of mercy were the central focus of the formation of new religious orders. They were a central activity of monasteries and dioceses. The modern age witnessed the growth of new religious congregations and institutions concerned with social needs. Social problems were at the center of papal encyclicals dealing with industrialization and the modern economic order.

Communality: The works of mercy were understood as a task of the Christian community and not simply as obligations of individual Christians. This communal emphasis does not belittle the significance of the individual Christian's commitment to the works of mercy as much as it underscores that the Christian community has on a local, diocesan, and more universal level a communal responsibility to deal with the needs and ills entailed in the works of mercy.

Societal critique: The history of Christian praxis displays a twofold relation to the works of mercy. On the one hand, this commitment to the works of mercy within the Christian community took place through various forms of institutionalization within the churches themselves. In other words, the churches themselves performed works of mercy. On the other hand, beside this constant practice of the works of mercy, there was the awareness that ecclesial forms of institutionalization were insufficient and that societal programs needed to be encouraged or criticized in relation to their social effects. This aspect is evident in the episcopal criticism of the Roman Empire's tax policy, the requirement of medieval councils that bishops supervise the adequacy of the medieval city's social programs, and, finally, the criticism of the negative effects of modern industrialization and the discrepancy between the rich and the poor results in a critique of economic systems and political programs in papal encyclicals, Catholic social teaching, political and liberation theologies.

2. Two Transformations

Alongside these three constants, two significant transformations relate to specialization and increased governmental involvement. The first is that the increased *specialization* in carrying out the works of mercy does not emerge at once, but its roots lie in the medieval period, and even earlier. This tendency of increased specialization leads to a bureaucratization and professionalism of social services within the modern period. The predominance of these tendencies of bureaucratization and professionalization within contemporary society needs to be critically and theologically examined.

The *increased governmental role* in regard to social assistance and welfare is another transformation. Social assistance became increasingly transferred from the Church and religious organizations to society. At first, the civic responsibility was local, but, increasingly, more and more elements of social assistance became the provenance of the State during the modern period. Moreover, the scope and range of the social services became much more extensive. This increased involvement of the State with regard to social welfare takes place, not only because of the increased amount of needs, but also because of a fundamental shift in attitude toward poverty and unemployment.

A theological interpretation of the works of mercy should, therefore, take into account both the three constants and the two transformations. Such a theological interpretation needs to articulate the centrality, communality, and social-critical dimension constant within the Christian tradition, and it also needs to reflect on the increased professionalized specialization and the increased governmental role in social assistance. This survey of the constants and transformations within the tradition provides the context for the next step in our analysis: an examination of two representative interpretations of the works of mercy, those of Thomas Aquinas and Juan Vives.

III. THEOLOGICAL INTERPRETATION AND THE WORKS OF MERCY

Thomas Aquinas represents the medieval theological understanding of the works of mercy, whereas Juan Vives presents an understanding that emerged in the Renaissance and could be considered a "prototype" of modern theological conceptions. The differences between these two, taken as "ideal-types," show differences in the assessment and approach to the works of mercy. These differences bring to the fore some basic issues in explicating a theological interpretation of the works of mercy.

Thomas Aquinas's exposition of the works of mercy not only exemplifies a significant medieval theological interpretation of the works of mercy, but it also exemplifies a conception that has strongly influenced traditional Roman Catholic theology. A brief examination of his interpretation of the works of mercy will, therefore, show the following: First, it will clarify not only medieval, but also traditional, Catholic theological understanding of the works of mercy. Such a clarification should eliminate some misunderstandings of traditional Roman Catholic interpretations of the works of mercy. Second, it enables us to show the difference between the medieval horizon and our own contemporary horizon.

A. THE WORKS OF MERCY IN THOMAS AQUINAS

The traditional Roman Catholic and medieval interpretations of the works of charity and benevolence are often misunderstood. One author, for example, recently asserted:

> The traditional attitude of the past had valued the giving of alms as an act of charity. The dominant Christian view until then had defined the act of charity, not primarily as a means of helping those who needed help, but rather as a means by which the virtuous exercised one of their religious faculties. The poor and dependent existed so that the well-to-do and the able would be in a position to demonstrate their own goodness.[23]

This interpretation of the traditional works of mercy as opportunities for the display of virtue rather than as occasions for the assistance of the needy is a frequent charge and a typical misunderstanding. There do indeed exist significant differences between traditional and modern views of the works of mercy, but these must be carefully analyzed and their nuances understood.

Thomas followed the traditional division of the works of mercy into corporal and spiritual works—two sets of seven. The seven corporal works of mercy can, in medieval Latin, be briefly expressed in verb form as: *visito, poto, cibo, redimo, tego, colligo, condo* (visit, give drink, nourish, ransom, clothe, welcome, and bury). Six of the seven stem from Matthew 25: 35; the seventh, from the Book of Tobias 1: 21; 2: 4-49.[24] In the *Summa Theologica,* Thomas further divided the works of mercy according to the type of need: internal corporal needs (to feed the hungry and to quench the thirsty), the external corporal needs (to clothe the naked and to give shelter to the homeless), and needs caused by special occasion (to visit the sick and to ransom the captive). The spiritual works of mercy entail the giving of instruction and the giving of counsel to those intellectually in need, the comforting of those in need of comfort, and, against inordinate acts, reproving, pardoning, and bearing another's burden.

1. Theological Virtue of Charity Vs Social Virtue of Justice

Thomas's theological treatment of the works of mercy displays two salient features that show the difference between Thomas's horizon and our own. *First,* the works of mercy are among theological virtues, that is, they belong to those virtues by which humans are ordered to God. Mercy does not belong to the cardinal moral virtues which affect social life and include temperance, justice, prudence, and fortitude. This ordering of mercy appears perplexing to our contemporary horizon that views the works of mercy as a social virtue, that is, ordered to our relation to other human persons, rather than to God. An interpretation of Thomas should adequately comprehend the meaning and significance of his claim that the works of mercy belong to the theological virtues, ordering human life to God, in order to avoid the misunderstanding and criticism that medieval theology saw mercy more as an opportunity for becoming virtuous rather than for helping the needy.

The *second* salient feature—one closely related—is the differentiation of the works of mercy from the virtue of justice. Almsgiving as a theological virtue belongs to charity rather than to justice. In his treatment of the works of mercy, Thomas distinguished the virtue of almsgiving from that of liberality. Whereas mercy belongs to the virtue of charity, liberality (which is contrasted to avarice or prodigality) is both distinct from justice and yet a part of justice. Thomas distinguished mercy from justice because mercy does not give to another person what is that person's due, but rather what is one's own. Nevertheless, mercy is related to justice insofar as it is directed to others and is concerned with external matters.[25] In contrast to liberality, beneficence and mercy flow from a certain affection. Hence, the works of mercy belong to the virtue of charity. Liberality, however, involves money that one gives, not just to friends, but to those whom he knows not. One does so if one is not a lover of money. Thomas's treatment differs from the opinion of his predecessor, Alexander of Hales, who, in his *Summa,* considers the works of mercy to belong to the virtue of justice.[26] Thomas's view also requires a nuanced interpretation. Such linkage does not imply that almsgiving is only a counsel and not a precept. Almsgiving is a precept; we are indeed commanded to give alms. Indeed, Thomas quotes Ambrose to the effect, "For in him who dies of hunger: if thou hast not fed him, thou hast slain him."[27] Whoever fails to give alms will be judged by God as worthy of damnation.

2. Interpreting Thomas's Theological View

The two assertions that mercy is a theological virtue and that it is a part of charity rather than justice need to be properly interpreted. Thomas's theological justification for the works of mercy shows the interrelation between the two assertions. It is often argued that Thomas gives a twofold justification: the divine command of love for the neighbor and a natural law argument about the right use of property.[28] Such an interpretation overlooks two important aspects. *First,* it has to explain its nature as a theological virtue. Since theological virtues are ordered toward God, an interpretation should explain the way the love of neighbor relates to the love of God. *Second,* Thomas's argument is not simply a natural law or a social argument about the correct use of goods, as it is a theological argument that the goods of the earth are God's. They properly belong to God as the creator. Consequently, although some persons have more goods than others, they do not have an absolute ownership of the goods, for that ownership belongs to God. In taking care of one's neighbor in need, one is distributing God's creation and goods to those who are in need.[29] The ownership of goods as well as the use of goods do not simply and exclusively belong to the individual alone, but to others and those in need. Such a view of ownership and distribution differs from the contemporary notions with the language of rights and entitlements. Almsgiving involves giving not what one owes to the needy. Yet, one can not refrain from almsgiving, not only because the Gospel commands us to love our neighbor, but also because the goods of the earth are God's goods and should be distributed to those who need them.

This linkage between God's ownership of the goods of the earth and the works of mercy brings to the fore the Christian conviction expressed in Christian liturgy. The presentation of gifts at the Eucharistic service embodies in liturgical practice the Christian belief that mercy toward the needy expresses the love of God. The goods of God's creation owed to God were distributed to those in poverty. It brings to the fore the biblical belief that almsgiving to the poor is at the same time an offering to God.[30] The link between the love of neighbor and the love of God also provides the linkage between charity and justice within Thomas's theology. Charity envisions the good of one's neighbor. One loves one's neighbor with the love and in the love that one has for God. Justice, however, refers to the object of possession.[31] Therefore, there is not a contrast, but a correlation.

B. A RENAISSANCE CONTROVERSY ABOUT THE WORKS OF MERCY

During the sixteenth century, pauperism became a fact of urban life. A series of bad harvests in the first quarter of the century led to a deterioration of the availability of food. In the third decade of the century, the bad harvest extended throughout all of Europe. In places, the exporting of wheat was forbidden. In some places, scarcely three to five percent of the population had reserves of wheat. A profound crisis was taking place in Europe. The agriculture was not able to take care of the demographic growth. A recession extended to commerce and finance. Villages were no longer able to provide employment for the handworkers. There were widespread malnutrition, famine, and the resulting illness. The popular revolts in Germany (1525-26) and in Spain (1520-21 and 1525-26) indicate the level of social unrest. These changes led to an increased immigration to the cities, but the cities were no longer able to integrate such a massive influx of people without means of support.

1. The Prohibition of Begging and New Social Policy

Various cities took measures to deal with the problem. Amiens decided to expel beggars who had newly immigrated so that they could take care of their own poor. After much debate,

Paris decided to limit the access of "poor foreigners" to the city, to provide work for their own unemployed in public works, and to create an institution of "Aumône générale" to take charge of the assistance to the poor. The prevalence of epidemics and the fear of their spread through the immigrant poor, who suffered not only malnutrition, but illness, led Venice, along with some other cities, not only to order their expulsion, but also to isolate them within certain quarters of the city.[32]

In 1525, Ypres, a city in Flanders, outlawed begging within the city. Such an ordinance might remind us of recent ordinances prohibiting begging in public places in North America, such as, the subways in New York, the Federal Reserve Building in Philadelphia, and the National Airport in Washington, D.C. Ypres's prohibition, however, was a much more wide-reaching and influential decision. Its prohibition of begging sought at the same time to reform the practices toward the poor and needy. Moreover, it sought to centralize the care of the poor, for Ypres not only outlawed begging, but it also organized a municipal form of assistance for those truly poor. The city itself assumed the complete responsibility for the organization of public assistance. It created a fund to cover the financial costs of administering such assistance, and it established functionaries who were to take on responsibilities for the poor. They were, so to speak, to take on the role of parents to the poor insofar as they were to concern themselves not only with their care, but also with their education and instruction.

This ordinance set into motion other ordinances during the Renaissance. The Emperor Charles V passed an ordinance throughout the Empire that outlawed begging conditionally. One could beg if one had a certificate from the pastor testifying to one's poverty, and this gave rise to fierce theological debates about the social and political care of the needy.[33] The ordinance led other cities to consider similar ordinances. The city of Bruges had asked the humanist, Juan Vives, for his advice regarding such an ordinance. Vives responded with a work entitled, *On the Support of the Poor (De subventione pauperum, sive de humanis necessitatibus)*. This work, published in 1526, dealt not only with the issue of begging and almsgiving to beggars, but it was a complete treatise on the problem of poverty.[34] It consisted of two parts. Part One dealt with the causes of poverty, the obligations toward the poor, and the various types of help. Of these, the most important was education because it trains people for work and encourages their self-worth. Part Two dealt with the task of the city leadership in regard to the poor. It concerned the municipal regulations of begging and of the care for the poor.

Historians have debated both Ypres's ordinances and Vives's work as well as their interrelation.[35] Since Vives had been asked for a written assessment precisely at the time that the proposed ordinance was under discussion, some presume he influenced it, whereas others assume that he was influenced by it. Regardless of such debates, his book is important because it brings to expression the very ideas and principles that underlie Ypres's ordinances. Its attitude toward poverty as well as its remedies display a signifying transformation of mentality. Juan Luis Vives warned that poverty often led to disorder, crime, disease, and immorality. Since the charitable works of mercy were, in addition to being a Christian precept, a practical concern, it was necessary for city officials to be concerned with the problem of poverty, its causes and its consequence. Vives urged city officials to provide education and work for the poor because idleness and poverty led to bad habits. Both Ypres's ordinances and Vives's book mark what could be called a turning point in the social, religious, and political interpretation of poverty and the way to deal with it. This turning point became the center of a theological debate.

2. The Theological Issues of the Debate

The debate centered on the prohibition of begging: the reasons for the prohibition and the reasons challenging it. Many challenged the prohibition as contrary to natural law and against the Gospel commandment. Faced with such criticisms, the City Council at Ypres petitioned the theological faculty of the Sorbonne University for an official theological evaluation. Such a petition was a petition for an official ecclesial assessment, for, during the medieval period, theological faculties were considered the Magisterium within the Church.[36] Canon Law did not go into effect until it was approved by the theological faculty of the Sorbonne. Papal decisions were sent to the theological faculty for their evaluation.

On January 16, 1531, the faculty responded that the city's regulations were complex, useful, and curative. The city's regulations could be seen to be in harmony with the Holy Scriptures, the Apostles, and the Early Church.[37] Nevertheless, the faculty attached certain stipulations or conditions: cities had to implement the regulations with care; they should not implement the regulations so as to harm the poor; the prohibition of begging should leave no one in need. If their funds can not take care of all the poor, then the cities should not prohibit those whom they could not help from begging. They should allow and encourage the rich and others to give freely to the poor. Moreover, cities should not take away property from the Church in order to take care of the poor. Mendicant orders should still be allowed to beg in order to collect for the poor. Finally, cities should be careful lest their regulations result in the poor within neighboring and less well off towns falling into extreme need.

A debate took place between a Franciscan and a Dominican theologian. In 1545, Juan de Medina, a Franciscan, published *De la orden que en algunos pueblos de España se ha puesto en la limosna para remedio de los verdaderos pobres,* in defense of the new legislation.[38] Domingo Soto, a Dominican, wrote *Deliberaccion en la causa de los pobres,* a critique of the laws (Salamanca, 1545).[39] Medina defended the new social rules with the argument that the law is not really so new because the Council of Tours already had something similar. If one gives alms only because of forceful begging, one does not gain merit. He argued instead that "it is better to sufficiently care for the poor than to have compassion on them."[40] The new legislation has many advantages: equality of income in contrast to mixed chance depending on one's success at begging, better care for children whose parents no longer needed to beg in order to provide for them.

In 1571, at the University of Ingolstadt, two Jesuits, Theodor Pelten and Adam Tanner, held a disputation on the matter of the works of mercy. Published in 1572, the disputation, entitled *De tertia et postrema satisfactionis parte,* reaffirmed the traditional view of mercy as integral to charity:

> Charity is the highest virtue; its genuine offspring is mercy, its grandchild, alms; the latter includes the participant attitude as well as the donation. It belongs to the perfection of almsgiving that the giver does not donate anything that he needs either for himself or for his family (order of love), furthermore nothing inappropriate (for example, jewels) and only donates to those really poor.[41]

Nevertheless, it went also beyond the tradition. In this debate, Pelten and Tanner agreed that the cities can reject immigrant beggars; where they disagreed is about the prohibition of begging by those already living in the cities. Pelten was much more critical of those regulations prohibiting such begging, whereas Tanner defended them.

The texts display some negative attitudes toward beggars. Not only are criminals unworthy of alms, but also those who are lazy or concerned to keep their skin soft (*"ut mollius cutem curent"*) or use their poverty as an excuse for robbing and injuring others.[42] Pelten prefers that the freedom to beg be preserved, but he grants that cities have the right to outlaw begging if they provide other opportunities for the poor. Tanner argues much more strongly that cities have the right to reject beggars and even to prohibit persons from begging if they are not in extreme need.

What emerges in this period and in these debates is a changed attitude, not only toward begging, but also toward poverty. Begging is not viewed as a virtue, but almost as a vice. It urged that no one should beg because of laziness and that vagrants should be brought to work. Children should be educated and should be trained so that, when they grow up, they will not have to beg. Vives places humanist concerns and pedagogical goals in the forefront. Moreover, these attitudes come to dominate. The attitude toward poverty radically changes in the sixteenth and seventeenth centuries. Poverty becomes increasingly viewed as an evil. Its eradication becomes increasingly a social goal. Such a transformed view of poverty came to dominate, not only the Renaissance and the Enlightenment critics of religion, but also the churches themselves, where social programs to eradicate poverty were articulated out of religious motivation.[43]

C. THE CHANGED THEOLOGICAL VIEW TOWARD ALMSGIVING

In the medieval period, religious attitudes towards the works of mercy, almsgiving, and care of the poor correlated with the societal conditions of persons belonging to different ranks and orders. During the Renaissance, the debate surrounding the prohibition of begging shows a different attitude toward begging and toward poverty. The debates were partly theological and partly political. On the one hand, a genuine practical concern about helping the poor was present. On the other hand, there is a strong fear about the social order, economic plight, and political situation of the cities. These debates reveal the changed attitudes toward poverty and the poor. It is these attitudes, combined with changed social, economic, and political circumstances, that lead to a new view of almsgiving and the works of mercy.[44]

A theological shift takes place in regard to the works of mercy, and this theological shift takes place in part because of different attitudes toward poverty. The Enlightenment attitude continues this shift in its attempt to remove the cause of poverty. The issue becomes increasingly the avoidance of poverty, and the theological ethical issue becomes charity or justice: the way one relates the theological works of mercy to the issue of justice and the prevention of poverty. Although the change is significant, there

are some structural elements that are not so different. My interpretation of Thomas's position pointed out that charity toward
God and the understanding of God's lordship over the goods of
creation were such that it required a right and just use of goods.
The virtue of charity, ordering human love toward God, brings
to the fore a relation to the goods of the earth that brings charity
into association with justice.

The shift takes place because of changing social conditions
due to the accumulation of capital within the modern period
and because of the different "ideological" view of the nature of
poverty. In the early medieval period, the monasteries had a
surplus that could be distributed. In the Renaissance and modern period, the further development of trade and industry made
capital, rather than land, the means of caring for the poor. At
the same time, theoretic views of poverty played an important
role. Within the medieval period, the "poor" were considered a
particular "estate" or a specific class of persons that were the
object of mercy. In the Renaissance, the unemployed and poor
were looked upon as vagrants and parasites. The social policy
was to give them work. If the medieval policy had its limitations, for example, not all had access to the distribution of
goods, the requirement for work in the Renaissance eventually
led to abuses during the modern period with the establishment
of the hated "workhouses" in England. The limitations of both
historical situations should not overlook the major shift in mentality toward poverty between what characterized the medieval
period and what came to characterize the modern period. If
Francis of Assisi could interpret his voluntary poverty as the
best way to follow Christ and express a relation to God, within
modernity Vincent de Paul underscores the dangers and evils of
poverty. Although both were concerned with helping the poor,
their different attitudes represent distinct views of poverty. This
shift and change become evident in the Renaissance debates
about the prohibition of begging.

IV. SOCIETAL EVOLUTION AND THE WORKS OF MERCY

Any theological interpretation of the works of mercy should
consider their social and political context. Changes in the organization of society, its structure and its regulation, have pro-
foundly affected the role and function of the works of mercy
within society. These are evident within the history of Christianity. Nevertheless, a macro description of societal changes in
relation to the works of mercy provides a broader context for

both the changes in the history of Christian praxis and the different theological interpretation.

A. SOCIAL EVOLUTION AND THE WORKS OF MERCY

Societies change, and social and political structures evolve over time, often becoming much more complex. Attempts to discuss social change or social evolution are sometimes questionable, especially when such changes are unfortunately placed into a progressive evolutionary scheme that is both rigid and evaluative. Rigid conceptions often overlook the overlapping and intersecting of earlier and later forms of development and the fact that a multiplicity of forms coexist. An evaluative assessment often falsely assumes that what is later is practically and morally more advanced. Such rigid and evaluative assessments were often a part of Victorian or Social-Darwinian approaches to religion and social evolution. Notwithstanding these reservations, such a typology underscores that the works of mercy and works of social assistance need to be conceived of differently within different contexts.

A survey of the changes and differences in social assistance in the course of societal evolutions has significance for the function and role of the works of mercy. One helpful example is the use of "system analysis" to relate social welfare to societal complexity.[45] Niklas Luhmann, a German sociologist, applies a system-theoretic modification of Talcott Parsons' functionalist approach to society and has looked at the works of mercy from this perspective. His analysis, not uncontroversial, needs to be complemented by a hermeneutical and critical theoretical approach to society.[46] Nevertheless, it does underscore significant differences among agrarian societies, highly cultivated societies, and modern societies, especially the modern industrialized West.[47] Each has distinctly characteristic approaches to social assistance.

Archaic and less developed *agrarian* societies are characterized by mutual assistance and reciprocal help. The assistance is primarily based on proximity of relationship of kinship, village, tribe, et cetera. Mutual assistance is given in the expectation of reciprocity. The assistance overcomes the contingencies of health, food supply, weather, environment, disasters, et cetera. Though some specialized help does exist — for example, medicine or magic — the help is primarily characterized by mutual reciprocity. It is often motivated by the possibilities that situations can be reversed or by the need to mutually withstand the rigors of the environment.

Complex societies are characterized by a division of labor in agriculture, industry, and trade. Political sovereignty has become much more differentiated, and the societal organization has become much more structured. Likewise, social assistance and welfare are also characterized by the increased societal division of labor. A professional group of helpers develops — doctors, lawyers, social workers, nurses — as well as professional organizations and institutions. One no longer expects reciprocity and immediacy in the return of help. Instead, money is used to purchase help.

Modern societies are characterized by a further complexity and organization. Attempts are made at the societal level to overcome help. Unemployment insurance should take care of those without work; disability insurance should address those too sick and disabled to work; social security should provide financial support for those too old or feeble to work. Welfare and medicare should address basic medical needs, and food stamps programs should supplement low income so that persons do not go hungry. These are societal systemic arrangements which are designed to take over much of the role of the works of mercy.

This sketch of societal change should not be misinterpreted so as to suggest that modern society, or even modern American society, has adequately solved the problems of needs that traditionally have called for the works of mercy. Quite the contrary, the recent decade gives evidence of dysfunctions and distortions. The wealthy five percent of the nation has benefitted enormously from tax cuts, whereas the poor have been victims of federal budget cuts that have handed down social programs to the states, and state budget cuts have transferred programs to local communities — all unable to meet some of the most pressing social needs. The wealthy have often insulated themselves in small, rich, suburban communities. The shift to local aid has thereby led to a further impoverishment of the poor.[48]

Instead, this sketch points to the need for an analysis of the structural organization of modern society in attempting through social programs to take over much of what in traditional societies would have been covered by the works of mercy. This systemic transformation in society raises the question: what is the role of the works of mercy within modern society? What role do the works of mercy have within a society that has organized social programs to deal with the issues involved in them? Do they deal with the inadequacies of the societal programs? Do they deal with needs that the social programs miss? Do they have a complementary role, or do they have a new and specific role? These questions become especially acute when we look at patterns of contemporary social organization.

B. MODERN SOCIAL ORGANIZATION AND THE WORKS OF MERCY

These questions need to be raised within the context of an analysis of modern society and its organization. Five characteristics of modern society are significant for the interpretation of the role of the works of mercy: bureaucratization, professionalism, monetarization, client-centeredness, and colonization of the life-world.

1. Bureaucratization of Social Policy

Within contemporary society, social welfare has become bureaucratized, and the distribution of social assistance entails multiple decisions. The first decision regards the *choice of social policy*. A nation or state has to decide for a particular social policy and for specific social programs. For example, countries can decide whether and what kind of national health insurance they want to implement. Though most industrial nations have decided for a national health insurance, the United States and South Africa are two exceptions. In the United States, current debates about the costs, amount, and eligibility for medicare, disability insurance, food stamps, help with housing, length of unemployment insurance are just a few of the debates about social policy in regard to the needy and indigent.

In addition, an *administrative decision* centers on the concrete application of social policy and practical guidelines of the social policy. An established bureaucracy deals with the administration of the guidelines. If persons are needy and should be covered by the social policy, but do not fit the concrete guidelines, then they do not receive assistance. The administrative bureaucracy has an impersonal structure and is ruled by guidelines that exclude personal and individual considerations of cases that do not fit the administrative guidelines.

Finally, the needy themselves must make a *decision of application* for social assistance. Do they know about the program? Do they have the concrete knowledge of the program or the possibility to apply, and/or are they even willing to apply for social assistance? For example, concrete reasons exist why homeless people do not want to enter shelters for the homeless. Or recently, as in the case of unemployment insurance, reasons exist that discourage applications. For instance, during the recent freeze in California, many farm workers lost their jobs. They could apply for unemployment benefits, but many immigrants decided they would endure the hardship because of regulations restricting those who have received welfare or unemployment benefits from becoming citizens of the United States. If they went on welfare, they might lose their chance at naturalization.

This multiple decision making opens social programs to dysfunctioning in regard to each of the decisions. Political influence and power often determine the formation of social policy. Groups with stronger political clout have a greater influence upon social policy than do groups who are in need, but who are without power. Entitlements are much more easily preserved — even if no longer needed — than they are obtained. Consequently, groups having a larger share of votes can more easily retain entitlements than groups without such a large share can obtain these. Other groups — for example, needy immigrant workers — lacking political clout or financial resources are at a disadvantage. In addition, the structures of bureaucratic organization also can lead to dsyfunctioning. Bureaucratic decision making is often highly organized and regulated so that whether an individual fits the regulations and is eligible may be so rigidly determined that many in need may not fit. Finally, limited access to information about assistance or its conditions might prevent many from receiving assistance. The needy may lack the educational resources or the financial ability to have access to the requisite information. The problems involved in each of these three types of decisions force one to ask what role do individual and Christian communities have — despite the social programs or, more precisely, because of the specific nature of social programs within contemporary society.[49]

2. Professionalization of Social Services

A major characteristic of modern society is increased professionalization.[50] This professionalization takes place in regard to the institutionalization of social work within society as well as within the churches. Social services are effective through institutional planning and professional training. There is an increasing differentiation of the works of mercy so that competencies become increasingly limited to narrow specializations. Personal commitment or natural inclination does not suffice, but one needs training to develop specific skills and to perform adequately specific tasks.

Specific vocations to specific forms of social care have existed for centuries, but a significant development takes place in the rise of modern professionalization. This professionalization entails not only the special training for a specific profession, but also the development of distinctive judgments and values. Modern professionalization has the distinguishing characteristics that technical competence and professional status are primarily defined in relation to a limited and particular skill, role, and field of knowledge.[51] It is not so much the general character or virtue of the person as it is the expertise in a given area that makes one a professional.

The professionalization of social work often requires that the social workers develop "professional attitudes" of distance and objectivity in their social engagement. Moveover, emotional elements should often be eliminated or objectified so that the assistance can be provided with impartiality and with a balanced judgment. The success of their social assistance and professional intervention should be subject to controlled measurement and assessment.[52] The limitation of professionalization to a specific skill and to a type of limited objectivity has given rise to the contemporary critique of professionalization. Though professionalization has led to an increased development of specific and diverse skills, it has not necessarily led to a holistic approach to social ills and problems.

3. Monetarization of Social Welfare

Along with the bureaucratization and professionalization of social services, a certain monetarization of social welfare takes place within modern societies.[53] Social welfare needs are met primarily through monetary payments. The unemployed, disabled, sick, and elderly are predominantly assisted to a large extent through insurance programs or governmental programs that provide them with the money to purchase social services. The unemployment check, the food stamp, social security benefit are all monetary benefits.

Such monetarization of social welfare fits within a market society and has advantages as well as disadvantages. The monetarization allows a certain amount of consumer choice in obtaining concrete services. Moreover, the monetary payment allows a degree of anonymity and self-respect for the needy person who is then not dependent upon direct personal assistance, but is provided with the means to purchase services. At the same time, it has the disadvantage that needs are quantified and measured in terms of this quantification. One attempts to measure the money required to take care of a specific need. Non-monetary factors, such as loneliness, self-respect, and self-estimation, cannot come within the calculus of such an approach. The non-personalization allowing anonymity is, at the same time, often not capable of satisfying these particular needs.

4. Social Work and a Therapeutic Client-Centeredness

A distinction is often made between social work and social policy because each of them stems out of two different traditions.[54] Social policy stems from the worker movement and has been concerned with issues of equity, just wages, working conditions, social benefits, and social security. Social work stems from an individualized tradition of health care and psychological care. Consequently, social work tends to be much more "therapeutically oriented." This term, used in its broadest sense, refers to the development of a relation to a person as a client in need of care and improvement, as if there is something wrong with individuals in a particular social situation that needs to be remedied. Hence, so it is thought, persons need to be made more self-reliant, independent, and self-empowered in order to deal with their social situation of need as if this need stemmed from their own deficiency, rather than from the dysfunctioning of social and economic systems.

5. Colonialization of the Life-World

Jürgen Habermas has advanced the thesis that in modern societies the life-world has become colonized insofar as society is primarily steered through the media of money and power (bureaucratic power).[55] Modern societies are steered, not by decisions based upon public discourse and discursive consent about substantial values, but, rather, in relation to money and bureaucratic power. The dominance of these media within the decision making of modern society has led to a certain deformation of the life-world with regard to substantive values. This thesis of colonialization is different from the thesis of secularization. Whereas the secularization thesis argues that religious values have become secularized, the colonialization thesis implies a deformation of decision. The generalization of values with modern society, a more appropriate description than secularization, encounters a society steered by the media of money and bureaucracy. The result is that these values are often not adequately brought into public discourse and into policy decision making.

In recent literature, feminist philosophers and political theorists have sought to explicate the notion of the colonialization of the life-world in relation to the welfare system in the United

States.[56] They note that within the welfare system certain needs are institutionalized, especially the needs of males, whereas other needs, those of women and other underprivileged groups, are suppressed. This discrepancy in the institutional patterns of welfare is explained as such: "The welfare system's interpretation of women's needs is distorted in part by its own requirement that those needs be 'translated' into the standardized, quantifiable form that can be dealt with by the administration."[57] In addition, there is also discrimination between recipients of unemployment and Social Security benefits, who are largely male and considered rightful recipients of aid, and recipients of AFDC (Aid to Families with Dependent Children), who are largely female and considered to be "dysfunctional" families with few rights and benefits. The woman's need for education and job training (so that she can one day earn a decent and sufficient wage) is treated, not as a need, but as a motivational interest.

Sets of problems concerned with social work seem today much more nuanced and much more difficult. It was often simply that the sick needed care or the sick were not strong enough to take care of themselves. Today, with the increasing role of State as well as private hospitals, questions emerge as to what is distinctive about a religious hospital or a Roman Catholic hospital. The issue of the care of the sick is replaced with the issue of the distinctive role of a religious or Christian hospital. The argument is that a religious hospital that is concerned about the holistic well-being of the patient is concerned about the interrelation between the medical and psychological, the physical and personal, the personal and religious dimensions of well-being. To the extent that health care is "secularized," or taken over by the State or society in general, to that extent the question of the religious dimension of health care and the special role of religious hospitals comes even stronger to the fore.

V. A THEOLOGICAL INTERPRETATION OF THE WORKS OF MERCY

The survey of the history of Christian praxis, the two theological discussions of the works of mercy, and the transformed societal structures of modern society brings us to the basic question as to the role of Christian communities in regard to the works of mercy within modern societies when modern social legislation attempts to take over much of what traditionally was performed by the Church under the rubric of the works of mercy. How do the practices and theological interpretations of the Christian tradition about the works of mercy inform contemporary theological reflection on the works of mercy under the situation of the transformations of modern society?

The practice of the works of mercy involves a complex set of issues. Moreover, the Christian tradition has brought obligation to the poor under the category of love and charity, but in ways that approximate the categories of justice. My analysis suggests that we have to theologically elucidate the values expressed in the works of mercy, especially their implied emphasis on the option for the poor and solidarity with victims. This solidarity has been elaborated through notions of charity and justice. It needs to be reformulated today in the light of an awareness of changed background assumptions about society and poverty, the retroductive warrants from experience, and an awareness of communities of discourse: voices of the homeless, voices of the sick and the ill that need to be heard within the ecclesial communities.

A. WORKS OF MERCY: JUSTICE OR CHARITY

The formulation of the works of mercy in terms of an alternative between charity or justice is inadequate to deal with the history of the works of mercy as well as with the meaning of justice. Such an alternative overlooks that the practice of justice, if it is to deal equally with persons, has to take into account their inequalities of talents, possessions, and status. Theories of justice have to deal with the historical differences between persons within society, and it is in dealing with these differences that crucial options in regard to a theory of justice come to the fore.

1. Liberal Justice and Difference Principle

Contemporary theories of justice, consequently, can be analyzed in relation to the way they take into account the disadvantaged and the needy within society. Whereas theorists like Robert Nozick emphasize individual rights and the possession of entitlements of those well-off who have earned these entitlements through education, effort, and labor,[58] other theorists, such as John Rawls and Jürgen Habermas, seek to take into account the disadvantaged. John Rawls develops two basic principles of justice.[59] The first concerns freedom and equal opportunity, and the second is known as the "difference principle." This difference principle means that those who are disadvantaged within society have the right to receive a greater proportion in order to make up for their disadvantage. One's disadvantage is not one's fault, and one's advantage is not one's sole effort. The difference principle exists in order to assure equality of opportunity.

Rawls argues, however, that it is reasonable to agree to such a double principle of justice. If we could imagine an "original position" in which no one would know what status or position he/she would be born into the world, he/she would choose a system of justice where all would be equal, and the disadvantaged would receive an extra assistance so that they could have equal opportunity. One employs, in fact, a very similar argument today with regard to catastrophic health care. Since a catastrophe can unexpectedly devastate the finances of anyone, well-to-do as well as poor, persons vote rationally when they vote to be taxed for it, since no one can know in advance whether he or she will become catastrophically ill. It is especially through the difference principle and its expansion that one can justify a political and social policy for the disadvantaged within society, both national and international.[60]

Rawls's position abstracts from concrete history and uses a hypothetical counter-factual thought-experiment in order to elucidate the relationship among the principles of equal freedom, equal opportunity, and the disadvantaged. Yet, we live in a concrete historical situation in which some have more entitlements and advantages than others do. The ahistorical nature of the original position as a justification for a difference principle belies the concrete historical existence of human nature and society. An alternative to this approach is Jürgen Habermas's theory of discourse ethics, with its explication of the transcendental and pragmatic nature of ethical discourse. Within such a conception, the complementary side of justice is solidarity.[61] Whereas justice deals with the equal freedom of individual persons, solidarity relates to the common welfare of consociates as well as the integrity of the common life. As Habermas underscores, "It is a question not so much of two moments that supplement each other as of two aspects of the same thing."[62] The interrelation among the notions of equal rights, solidarity, and common welfare is not simply a formal logical or ethical interrelation, but it is an interrelation historically rooted in a religious tradition and history with their vision of the individual's value in relation to a community and to God.

2. Christian Principle of Solidarity

The significance of reconstructing the integrity and tradition of the Christian teaching about the works of mercy and solidar-

ity with the poor and hungry become, at this point, an important issue. Abstract principles of justice find their complement
within a tradition of concrete moral discourse and practice.[63]
The Christian discourse and practice of the works of mercy underscore the principle of solidarity and a principle of all sharing
in the goods of God's creation. These principles of solidarity
and sharing come to the fore when one interprets the works of
mercy in relation to charity and justice.

The principle of solidarity has been a constant teaching
within Roman Catholic social teaching. Although the term "solidarity" stems from the language of liberation theologies and
critical social theory, a similar point has been expressed with
diverse images and concepts in recent Catholic social teaching.
John Paul II argues in his encyclical celebrating the century of
Pope Leo XIII's *Rerum Novarum* (1891) that Leo XIII used the
term "friendship"; Pope Pius XI, the term "social charity"; and
Paul VI, "civilization of love." The Pope equates the idea of "solidarity" and of "solidarity with the poor" with the implied intent
of the previous papal teaching.[64] A continuity does indeed exist,
though the categories of solidarity with the poor and option for
the poor bring to the fore a concrete social political commitment
that is not simply expressed in the ideas of friendship or civilization of love. The notion of solidarity underscores practical commitment to the disadvantaged, needy, and poor within a society.
Such a commitment underscores inner connection between love
and justice.

My point is that the practice and discourse of the works of
mercy bring a tradition of solidarity into public discourse. The
ethical choice of society, whether justice is conceived according
to a theory of entitlements or according to a "difference principle," is not simply a decision that can be justified through an
abstract rationality. Instead, it is a decision that is based on a
vision of humanity and the world. The Christian tradition envisions all humans as representing the divine and the goods of the
world as created by God for all. Such a vision has expressed the
traditional Christian teaching of the works of mercy. Such a vision entails an understanding of justice based, not on a theory
of entitlements, but on a difference principle that seeks to enable the disadvantaged and indigent to share in God's creation.

B. THE ROLE OF CHURCH COMMUNITIES AND THE WORKS OF MERCY

Christians have, throughout the history of Christianity,
viewed the works of mercy as central to the Christian commu-

nity. They are not simply obligations for individual Christians, but a responsibility and a task for the Christian community. This communitarian social responsibility is integral to the Christian tradition. The obligations of individuals to perform the works of mercy take place within the context of a community and its practice. Christian churches as communities of disciples express their communal solidarity through their commitment to the works of mercy.

From the small local community of early Christianity to the establishment of medieval and modern religious orders or lay confraternities, from the episcopal critique of Roman tax policies to the medieval concern about the social practice of cities, and to the papal criticism of industrialization and the split between developed and undeveloped countries, the works of mercy were understood as a task of the community, of its liturgy, its institutional organization, and its teaching and preaching. The works of mercy are constitutive of the Christian community. The question is not simply, what does one do as a good individual Christian, but also what does the Christian community as a community do in regard to the works of mercy? The above analysis implies, in my opinion, that the churches as communities have five distinct and complementary roles in regard to the works of mercy within modern society and its changed form of social assistance and societal welfare.

1. Societal and Political Critique

The emphasis, first developed by political theology and then by liberation theology, that the Church should exercise social and political criticism becomes important to the extent that political policy decisions often affect social programs and the needy.[65] It is also important insofar as the vision of society can be such that it is one based on entitlements or one based on difference principles. Hence, the role of churches within a society that takes over much of the traditional works of mercy is both to criticize inadequacies of social policy, especially to the extent that such social policy, often, does not sufficiently take into account the victims and voiceless of society.

2. Countering Dysfunctional Social Programs

The dysfunctioning of social programs and their administration is unavoidable. The imperative to reform the structures of society so that they become more just and to improve social programs so that they become more equitable and responsive to needs is also an imperative to avoid the utopian illusion of complete success. Since even the best social programs will be dysfunctional in some way, the need will exist for individuals and communities to be attentive to blind spots, weaknesses, and dysfunctioning of societies. The "politics" of social policy, its bureaucratization and systemic structure make this dysfunctioning a part of every historical society and pose problems and challenges that must be met.

Such dysfunctioning is often caused by the *de facto* parameters of the formation of the policy itself. It is often the case that governmental policy issues focus primarily on the allocation of resources for social services within the context or limits of encouraging corporate and national or regional economic growth. The basic goals are assumed and presupposed so that the discussion often concerns very narrow issues, such as the cost of a particular social program and its relation to the increase or reduction of a governmental deficit or in relation to an increase or decrease of taxes: "Policy has always been oriented to the best way to allocate the surplus for individual and collective consumption rather than the more central question of the best way to control the process to realize social needs and the full potential of human beings."[66]

3. Global Awareness in the Universal Church

Through an ironic twist of faith, a change of consciousness has taken place in Roman Catholicism. If one examines the history of Roman Catholicism for large periods of history, Roman Catholicism was largely limited to Europe. During the Middle Ages, it was Islam that could claim universality, for it expanded from Spain and Africa, from the Middle East, to Iran, Iraq, Turkey, and the borders of Europe. In comparison, Christianity was a European ghetto. Yet, Christianity understood itself as "catholic." Today, Christianity is much more aware of its particularity within humankind and the religions of the world. Yet today, Christianity exists more outside of the West than it does in Europe. The majority of Christians, and increasingly so, will come from the Third and Fourth worlds.

At the same time that Catholicism has become a world Church, the world has become local. Through telecommunication, every corner of the world can become immediately present to us. We can see people starving and dying before our very eyes. We can reach or travel to many areas of the world in hours or, at the most, in days. This immediacy brings to consciousness the unity of humankind. Everywhere in the globe, we encounter our fellow human, our fellow brother and sister. At the same time, we are aware of the unity of the eco-system; the fossil fuel that we burn affects not only our forests or our ozone layer, but also those in other parts of our globe.

Consequently, the question of who constitutes our neighbor has been altered, even though it is often argued that our neighbor is primarily our own countryman. For example, Richard Rorty writes in reference to the treatment of blacks in the United States: "Do we say that these people must be helped because they are our fellow human beings? We may, but it is much more persuasive, morally as well as politically, to describe them as our fellow *Americans* — to insist that it is outrageous that an *American* should live without hope."[67] Within the New Testament, "the least of the brethren" often referred to the members of the immediate Christian community. The quotes of brotherly love within the Johannine epistles referred almost exclusively to the members of the Christian community. The regulations of the Renaissance referred primarily to our village or our local community. Nor should it be simply the members of our religious community. But, it must include the unfortunate of the world, and it must especially include those of the Third and Fourth worlds.[68] These are affected by the way we live, and these are in need. The interlocking principles of charity and justice need to be extended globally.[69]

4. Holistic Practice

The specialization and fragmentation of the works of mercy often entail further departmentalization in health care. Consequently, the caring for the sick and terminally ill in hospitals requires a care that is much more than medical.[70] Serious illness disrupts normal daily life. It isolates persons from their families. It forces persons to confront their fragility and finitude. It often brings them face to face with the realization of death. The bureaucratization and monetarization of health care fail to adequately deal with such a situation. Disability benefits may provide a temporary substitute for salary; health insurance may take over the hospital bills. Yet, in each of these cases, what is needed is much more.

One could say the social program is successful if the need is met with monetary means. Yet, a person who is unemployed and cannot find employment undergoes a terrible loss of self-value and self-worth. A disabled person does not only need money, but also needs to realize his/her value as a person despite his/her disability. If someone is ill and hospitalized, that person may experience profound loneliness, separated from family and loved ones, concerned about future health. If the breadwinner of the family dies, a welfare check cannot provide the love and emotional support needed to live and to rear a family. Even where the social welfare system might be successful insofar as it meets needs with monetary benefits, there remains a personal and interpersonal need. Christian communities and Christians individuals, therefore, have the task of providing personal and communal relations, helping persons to find self-identity and self-worth.

5. Innovative and Alternate Models

It is important to underscore the importance of the Christian community's seeking to develop alternative models of life style. To be concerned about the hungry, poor, and sick is not only a matter of decisions for social programs — for taking care of persons neglected by these programs, and caring for them in a holistic fashion, but it is also an equally essential matter of the way we live. For example, the high consumption of meat uses up grain that might be available for others. The national use of wealth for elective or special medical services uses up wealth and financial resources that might more profitably go to poor individuals and countries lacking basic medical services. These examples can be multiplied.

In my opinion, John Paul II put his finger precisely on this problem in his recent encyclical when he wrote:

> It is therefore necessary to create lifestyles in which the quest for truth, beauty, and goodness and communion for the sake of common growth are the factors which determine consumer choices, savings and investments. In this regard it is not a matter of the duty of charity alone, that is, the duty to give from one's "abundance" and sometimes even out of one's needs in order to provide what is essential for the life of a poor person. I am referring to the fact that even the decision to invest in one place rather than another, in one productive sector rather than another, is always a moral and cultural choice.[71]

Choices involved in our very way of living, from choices of food and medical care to investment decisions, are moral choices that affect the poor in our own country as well as in other countries. The implication of the Pope's statement is significant for our understanding of the works of mercy. The limited resources within the world and the scarcity of goods make our own life styles increasingly a problem. Helping the hungry and poor, the naked and the thirsty is not simply a matter of giving from the surplus. Nor is it simply that which we can give or do when we give of our surplus to the poor and needy. Instead, it is an issue of the life that we live, the choices that we make, the food that we eat, the investments that we make because these affect the poor and disadvantaged. If we as Christians are to exercise that charity and justice proclaimed in the tradition's affirmation of the works of mercy, then we have to live an alternative life practice, one not based primarily on increased consumption of goods, but on the sensitivity that the goods of the earth are not ours alone. To so live is to take seriously the challenge placed before the Christian community by the Parable of the Last Judgment.

VI. CONCLUSION

Rather than a conclusion, I shall summarize briefly the points of my essay. First: the Scriptures present a challenge to us insofar as they make the works of mercy a criterion for salvation and for Christian identity. They equate works of mercy with the love of God and love of Christ. This biblical challenge remains today, but it becomes necessary to examine the works of mercy in the light of Christian tradition, contemporary society, and the experience of the Christian community.

Second: a theological perspective on the works of mercy requires more than a mere correlation between biblical symbols and contemporary questions. Instead, theology seeks to synthesize diverse elements. It seeks to interpret the integrity and ideals of the tradition, to consider the ongoing experience of Christian communities (retroductive warrants), to reflect on background assumptions about society (background theories), and to attend to the voices of the oppressed or poor, challenging our assumptions and self sufficiency (communities of discourse). We begin to articulate the Christian vision of the works of mercy when we take all four elements into account.

Even a brief analysis of the Christian tradition shows that the works of mercy have not been limited to acts of individual piety, but rather constitute the identity of the Christian community. Consequently, throughout its history, the Christian community has sought to incorporate the works of mercy within its liturgical life, to develop institutional forms appropriate to the exercise of the works of mercy, and has engaged in social and political criticism.

Third: our theological interpretation of the works of mercy considered two distinct treatments of the works of mercy: Thomas Aquinas's understanding of the works of mercy as belonging to the theological virtue of charity and the debate within the sixteenth century concerning the prohibition of begging. One is paradigmatic for medieval theological attitudes; the other becomes indicative of the emerging modern society. It would be false to simply equate the difference between the medieval and the modern to a difference between an emphasis on charity and an emphasis on justice. Instead, elements of justice pervade the medieval understanding of the works of mercy. What are different are the different conceptions of poverty and the changing economic and social conditions of society.

Fourth: modern society, with its policy of social welfare, involves a bureaucratization, professionalism, and monetarization of much of the needs traditionally covered by the works of mercy. This development, especially the colonialization of the life-world, does not eliminate the need for the Christian community's involvement within the works of mercy, but calls for new forms of social and political ministry.

Fifth: the contribution of the Christian churches consists in their articulation of the meaning of their tradition that emphasized the solidarity with the poor and oppressed within the context of a vision of justice for all. In addition, the churches exercise the works of mercy in ways that involve: societal and political critique, countering the dysfunctioning of social systems, awareness of the global context, developing holistic practice, and bringing forth alternate and innovative models of care.

NOTES

[1]James H. Cone, *The Pastor as Servant,* ed. Earl E. Shelp and Ronald H. Sunderland (New York: The Pilgrim Press, 1991), 64. (See 63-64 for the poem.)

[2]For an analysis of this text, see Johannes Friedrich, *Gott im Bruder: Eine methodenkritische Untersuchung von Redaktion. Ueberlieferung und Traditionen in Mt 25, 31-46* (Stuttgart: Calwer Verlag, 1977).

[3]See Martin Dibelius, *James: A Commentary on the Epistle of James,* revised by Heinrich Greeven (Philadelphia: Fortress, 1976), 39-50, 230-40. (See 50 for quote.)

[4]See Jeffrey Hadden, *The Gathering Storm in the Churches* (New York: Doubleday, 1969).

[5]See my essay, "The Social Mission of the Church," in *Dictionary of Roman Catholic Social Thought,* ed. Judith Dwyer (Collegeville, Minn.: Liturgical Press, 1992).

[6]For a fuller development, see Francis Schüssler Fiorenza, "Systematic Theology: Method and Tasks," in *Systematic Theology. Roman Catholic Perspectives,* ed. Francis Schüssler Fiorenza and John Galvin (Minneapolis: Fortress, 1991), 1: 3-91, and "The Crisis of Hermeneu-

tics and Christian Theology," in Sheila Greeve Davaney, ed., *Theology at the End of Modernity* (Philadelphia: Trinity Press, 1991), 117-40.

[7]See Francis Schüssler Fiorenza, *Foundational Theology. Jesus and the Church* (New York: Crossroad, 1983), 301-21.

[8]See Wilhelm Schneemelcher, "Der diakonische Amt in der alten Kirche," in Herbert Krimm, ed., *Das Diakonische Amt der Kirche,* 2d ed. (Stuttgart: Evangelische Verlagswerk, 1963), 61-105.

[9]Irenaeus IV, 18, 2.

[10]*First Apology,* #67.

[11]The translation of Daniel 4: 27 by the *New English Bible* illustrates more clearly a meaning of the text that is closer to Cyprian's use than is that of the *Revised Standard Version.* The *NEB* translation is: "Be advised by me, O king: redeem your sins by charity and your iniquities by generosity to the wretched. So may you long enjoy peace of mind."

[12]Cyprian, *On Works and Alms,* Section 20, in *Library of the Fathers,* Vol. III (Oxford: John Henry Parker, 1839).

[13]The literature on the works of mercy within the Medieval Church is often polemic or apologetic. Protestant historians often criticized the medieval period as over concerned with the merits of the individual giving the alms. The Enlightenment critique often criticized the medieval period as having a too unsystemic approach to poverty. Roman Catholic historians often focused their work in responding to these two criticisms and showing the "other side." Instead of a polemic or apologetic approach, the distinctiveness of its development should be seen within its social context.

[14]Wilhelm Liese, *Geschichte der Caritas* (Freiburg: Caritasverlag, 1922), 1: 222.

[15]See Paul Christophe, *Les pauvres et la pauvreté des origines au XVe siècle* (Tournai: Desclée, 1985).

[16]Jean Imbert, ed., *Histoire des hopitaux en France* (Toulouse: Privat, 1982).

[17]See Georg Ratzinger, *Geschichte der kirchlichen Armenpflege* (Freiburg: Herder, 1884), 281-94.

[18]Michel Mollat, *The Poor in the Middle Ages: An Essay in Social History,* trans. Arthur Goldhammer (New Haven: Yale University Press, 1986).

[19]Bronislaw Geremek, *La potence ou la pitié. L'Europe et les pauvres du Moyen Âge à nos jours* (Paris: Éditions Gallimard, 1978).

[20]Kate und Theodor Brandt, "Das Erbe des Pietismus Praxis der Kirche," in *Gemeinde in diakonischer und missionarischer Verantwortung,* ed. Theodor Schober and Hans Thimme (Stuttgart: Quell Verlag, 1979), 102-108.

[21]See Emanuel Chill, "Religion and Mendicity in Seventeenth-Century France," *International Review of Social History* 7 (1962): 400-25. For a slightly earlier time frame, see also Brian Pullen, *Rich and Poor in Renaissance Venice: The Social Institutions of a Catholic State to 1620* (Cambridge: Harvard University Press, 1971), and his essays, "Catholics and the Poor in Early Modern Europe," *Transactions of the Royal Historical Society* 5th ser., 26 (1976): 15-34.

[22]For a contrast between political and liberation theologies, see Francis Schüssler Fiorenza, "Political Theology and Liberation Theology: An Inquiry into Their Fundamental Meaning," in Thomas McFadden, ed., *Liberation, Revolution and Freedom* (New York: Seabury Press, 1975): 3-29.

[23]Nathan Irving Huggins, *Protestants Against Poverty: Boston Charities, 1870-1900* (Westport, CN: Greenwood, 1971), x-xi.

[24]See "La Doctrine Catholique de l' aumône, *Nouvelle Revue Théologique* 54 (1927): 5-36.

[25]*Summa Theologiae* II-II, 117, 5. The fifth article concerns whether liberality is a part of justice.

[26]See Part II.

[27]*Summa Theologiae* II-II, 32,6.

[28]Johann Foerstl, *Das Almosen. Eine Untersuchung über die Grundsätze der Armenfürsorge im Mittelalter und Gegenwart* (Paderborn: Ferdinand Schöningh, 1909).

[29]Cf. Léon Bouvier, *Le précepte de l' aumône chez Thomas d' Aquin* (Montreal: Studia Collegii maximi immaculatae conceptionis, 1935), and Paul Goreux, "L' aumône et le régime des biens," *Nouvelle Revue Théologique* 49 (1932): 117-31 and 240-54.

[30]See Klaus Berger, "Almosen für Israel," *New Testament Studies* 23 (1976/77): 180-204.

[31]See Bouvier, *Le précepte,* 186: "En résumé, le devoir de la charité se prend dans la personne du prochain, l'obligation de la justice, dans la chose même, l'objet de la possession."

[32]Geremek, La potence ou la pitié, 159-81.

[33]Henri Pirenne, *Histoire de Belgique* (Brussels, 1927), 3: 290. A considerable "ecumenical"debate within historical scholarship exists about the origin of this ordinance in relation to Catholic or Protestant thought and in regard to possible prototypes of the legislation in German cities.

[34]Vives's book was very popular, and both Spanish and Latin versions were distributed. For a Spanish edition of the text, see Juan Luis Vives, *Del socorro de los pobres, o de las necesidades humanes* (Madrid: Sucesores de Hernando, 1922).

[35]One historical debate has been a controversial theological debate between Roman Catholic and Protestant historians at the turn of the century: whether the Reformation or Roman Catholicism has done more development of social assistance in the sixteenth century. See Franz Ehrle, *Beiträge zur Geschichte und Reform der Armenpflege* (Freiburg: Herder, 1881). Today, the attention has shifted away from a focus on whether Protestant or Catholic influences were at work in Ypres to that of the influence of Renaissance humanism.

[36]Hubert Jedin, "Theologie und Lehramt," in Remigus Bämer, ed., *Lehramt und Theologie im 16. Jahrhundert* (Münster: Aschendorff, 1976).

[37]See Ratzinger, *Geschichte,* 443ff.

[38]Published in 18th century editions as *La charidad discreta practicada con los mendigos.*

[39]A Latin translation appeared two years later: *In causa pauperum deliberatio.*

[40]"es mejor quitar à los pobres de miserias que procurar ocasiones de compassion lasquales nuncan se pueden haver sin daño del proximo" (p. 64). Quoted from Liese, *Geschichte,* 1: 297.

[41]Liese, *Geschichte,* 1:300.

[42]Ibid., 1: 300-301.

[43]Robert Jutte, "Poor Relief and Social Discipline in Sixteenth-Century Europe," *European Studies Review* 11 (1981): 25-52.

[44]Liese, *Geschichte,* 1:303, suggests that social order is secondary to the desire to help the poor.

[45]Niklas Luhmann, *The Differentiation of Society* (New York: Columbia University Press, 1982).

[46]See the debate between Habermas and Luhmann in Jürgen Habermas and Niklas Luhmann, *Theorie der Gesellschaft oder Sozialtechnologie — Was leistet die Systemsforschung* (Frankfurt: Suhrkamp, 1971).

[47]Niklas Luhmann, "Formen des Helfens im Wandel gesellschaftlicher Bedingungen," *Soziologische Aufklärung:* 2. *Aufsätze zur Theorie der Gesellschaft,* 2d ed.(Cologne: Westdeutscher Verlag, 1971), 134-49, and "Die Organisationsmittel des Wohlfahrtstaates und ihre Grenzen," *Verwaltete Bürger — Gesellschaft in Fesseln,* ed. Heiner Geissler (Frankfurt: Ulstein, 1978), 112-20.

[48]See Robert B. Reich, "Secession of the Successful," *The New York Times Magazine,* 20 January 1991, Section 6.

[49]For a critical analysis of policy making, see the essays by Frank Fischer and John Forester, in John Forester, ed., *Critical Theory and Public Life* (Cambridge: MIT, 1985), 231-81.

[50]Talcott Parsons, "The Professions and Social Structures," in his *Essays in Sociological Theory,* rev. ed. (New York: Free Press, 1964), 34-49.

[51]For a critique of professionalization in general, see Donald A. Schön, *The Reflective Practitioner: How Professionals Think in Action* (New York: Basic Books, 1982), 3-69, and Burton Bledstein, *The Culture of Professionalism: The Middle Class and the Development of Higher Education in America* (New York: W. W. Norton, 1976), and Magali S. Larson, *The Rise of Professionalism: A Sociological Analysis* (Berkeley: University of California Press, 1977).

[52]See Veronica Kircher, "Gedanken zum Wandel des Selbstverständnisses christlicher Caritas in den Letzen Jahrzehnten," in Richard Völkl, ed., *Caritative Diakonie der Kirche* (Aschaffenburg: Paul Pattloch Verlag, 1976), 63-75.

[53]For monetarization, see Jürgen Habermas, *Theory of Communicative Action,* 2 vols. (Boston: Beacon Press, 1987).

[54]See, for example, the essays by Helge Peters, "Sozialarbeit im gesellschaftspolitischen Kontext," *Soziale Welt* 23 (1972): 41-53, and "Die politische Funktionslosigkeit der Sozialarbeit und die 'pathologische' Definition ihrer Adressaten," *Jahrbuch für Sozialwissenschaft* 20 (1969).

[55]Habermas, *Theory of Communicative Action,* vol. 2.

[56]Nancy Frazer, *Unruly Practices* (Minneapolis: University of Minnesota Press, 1989). See also, Kathy Ferguson, *The Feminist Case against Bureaucracy* (Philadelphia: Temple University Press, 1984), and Iris Marion Young, *Justice and the Politics of Difference* (Princeton: Princeton University Press, 1990).

[57]Jane Braaten, *Habermas's Critical Theory of Society* (Albany: State University of New York Press, 1991), 148.

[58]Robert Nozick, *Anarchy, State, and Utopia* (New York: Basic Books, 1974).

[59]John Rawls, *A Theory of Justice* (Cambridge: Harvard University Press, 1971). For a response to critics of Rawls's position, see Thomas W. Pogge, *Realizing Rawls* (Ithaca: Cornell University Press, 1989).

[60]For a discussion of the difference principle and political theology, see Francis Schüssler Fiorenza, "Politische Theologie und liberale Gerechtigkeits-Konzeption," in *Mystik und Politik. Johann Baptist Metz zu Ehren,* ed. Edward Schillebeeckx (Mainz: Matthias Grünewald, 1988), 105-17.

[61]Jürgen Habermas, "Justice and Solidarity: On the Discussion Concerning 'Stage 6,'" in Michael Kelly, ed., *Hermeneutics and Critical Theory in Ethics and Politics* (Cambridge: MIT Press, 1990), 32-52; Reprint of *Philosophical Forum* 21 (1989): 32-52.

[62]Ibid., 47.

[63]"The Church as a Community of Interpretation: Between Discourse-Ethics and Hermeneutical Reconstruction," in *Habermas, Modernity, and Public Theology,* ed. Don Browning and Francis Schüssler Fiorenza (New York: Crossroad, 1992), 65-90.

[64]See Pope John Paul II, *Centesimus Annus, Origins* (May 16, 1991), 10-11.

[65]See Johann Baptist Metz, *Faith in History and Society: Toward a Practical Fundamental Theology* (New York: Crossroad, 1980), and *The Emergent Church* (New York: Seabury, 1986).

[66]Paul Smith and Michael Judd, "American Cities: The Production of Ideology," in Michael P. Smith, ed., *Cities in Transformation* (Berkeley: Sage, 1984), 184.

[67]Richard Rorty, *Contingency, Irony, and Solidarity* (New York: Cambridge University Press, 1989).

[68]See Pope John Paul II, *Centesimus Annus, Origins* (May 16, 1991), 1-24.

[69]See Charles R. Beitz, *Political Theory and International Relations* (Princeton: University of Princeton Press, 1979).

[70]See Mary Collins and David Power, ed., *The Pastoral Care of the Sick, Concilium* 199/2 (Philadelphia: Trinity Press, 1991).

[71]Pope John Paul II, *Centesimus Annus,* 36.

The Works of Mercy: Feeding the Hungry

Suzanne C. Toton

I first began researching the problem of hunger in 1972. I was in graduate school then, and, for the first time, at least in my memory, the American public saw hunger on their TV screens. The response was not all that different from the response to the Vietnam War—we were horrified at the sight of such human misery. I do not remember rock concerts responding to famine in the Sahel then (although my 18 year old students assure me that there were some), but I do remember a flurry of activity. Activity that focused on eating less beef and eating more rice and beans. Popular then were books like *Diet For a Small Planet*. In some mysterious way, the food I did not eat was supposed to make its way into the bellies of starving African children. I remember books and articles by the Paddock brothers, Paul Erlich, and Garret Hardin that proposed hard-nosed solutions, based on triage or a life-boat ethic. Fortunately, Lester Brown came to the rescue with his book, *By Bread Alone*, that attributed hunger to both overpopulation and overconsumption. Georg Borgstrom made a wonderful contribution in *The Food and People Dilemma* by bringing into question the very definition of over-population and exposing the fact that it was in the interest of the affluent nations to define the term to their advantage. Finally, Susan George, Frances Moore Lappe, and the 1974 World Food Conference forced us to see that neither eating lower on the food chain nor forcing birth control on the Third World would solve the problem of hunger. The causes and cures for hunger were much more deep-rooted and complex.

The World Food Conference identified poverty as the root cause of hunger and called for a more just restructuring of the economic and political structures and systems that govern the relationship between the First World and the Third World.

73

I remember all too well Henry Kissinger's moral rhetoric at the World Food Conference, giving our nation's pledge that "no child would go to bed hungry by the end of the decade." Today, almost twenty years later, the Horn of Africa is gripped by famine. Moreover, by World Bank estimates, one billion people, that is, one in five people, are chronically malnourished world wide. Fifteen million children a year die of malnutrition and hunger-related diseases. And, the prospects for ending hunger today seem less promising than they have ever been. The question is why.

While the government and media would have us believe that we are a compassionate nation and that we respond to human suffering, I seriously question the depth of that compassion. The more I study the problem of hunger and poverty, the more convinced I am that there is no serious commitment or effort on the part of affluent nations or people to eliminate hunger. In fact, I would go so far as to say that the affluent nations of the world do not particularly care about poor and hungry people. The wasting of human life is seen as an unfortunate, but perhaps necessary, price that has to be paid to maintain the systems that traditionally have insured prosperity and political stability for some. The fact that people might suffer and starve is insignificant in the face of the systems that have to be preserved.

The tragedy of it all is that the churches are silent. It is not that they lack official statements criticizing unjust economic structures and systems and emphasizing the necessity of reforming them, but that they resist preaching the Gospel and witnessing to it in ways that are both public and political. Unless the churches are willing to channel the little compassion they have generated toward the hungry into effective political action, they must be seen as accomplices in the economic and political systems that perpetuate hunger.

In the pages that follow, I would like to examine one of the mechanisms through which First World charity flows to the Third World. I would like to focus, in particular, on one institution, the International Monetary Fund. I believe it can be easily demonstrated that its policies are geared primarily toward maintaining the world banking system as we know it and that increased hunger and poverty are their by-products. I want to do this for a number of reasons: 1) for those who see charity or assistance as a solution to the problem of hunger, to show that charity is itself political, 2) to add my voice to the voice of others who never tire of telling us that hunger cannot be attributed to drought or overpopulation, but is fundamentally rooted in economic and political systems, and 3) to do what I can to convince the churches and all who profess the Christian faith that matters of life and death are decided, not only in the private, but also in the public and political realm. To deny or ignore this fact today is to risk being on the side of death.

In his book on hunger in Africa, Lloyd Timberlake writes that in 1985 the media publicized the fact that 30 million Africans were starving because of drought.[1] But, in a normal year 100 million people's lives in Africa are threatened by hunger. The 30 million are not added to the 100 million; they are simply the most vulnerable, usually the elderly and children. When the media cover hunger, they focus on weather and only rarely on politics or economics. Politics enters into their coverage only when governments block or divert the emergency grain. But, hunger does not happen all of a sudden. The drought is merely the triggering event that pushes over the brink those whose economic and political situation is most precarious. After all, the more affluent nations have had droughts, but the death toll has never reached Africa's proportions. While we associate drought with Africa and want to believe that its hunger is due to drought, the fact of the matter is that the majority of African nations are desperately poor and deeply in debt. As a whole, Africa's foreign debt since 1972 has grown faster than that of any other region in the Third World. I would like to argue that hunger, poverty, and debt are all related. And, because they are, feeding the hungry today requires that we attend to them.

Most Americans are under the impression that international aid is simply given, that is, that it is transferred to the Third World in the form of outright grants. That simply is not the case. Seventy-five percent of the assistance transferred to the Third World from the First World is in the form of loans. These loans must be paid back to their donors at interest, and most of them come with conditions or strings attached. Another popular belief is that aid is humanitarian, that it goes to the poorest countries. Again, this is not the case. Most of the foreign assistance transferred to the Third World goes to political allies for political, military, or economic purposes. Take the United States, for example. In 1989, the lion's share of U.S. aid went to Israel which received three billion dollars. Egypt received 2.4 billion dollars; Pakistan, 581 million; Turkey, 563 million; the Philippines, 479 million; and El Salvador, 394 million. Ethiopia, which was gripped by famine, received four million dollars.[2]

Not only is foreign assistance not aimed at the poorest countries, but the bulk of it is not even aimed at relieving human misery. Using the United States again as an example, one notes that, since 1981, more military and military related assistance has been sent to every region of the world than development or emergency relief assistance has.

Finally, lest we think that the Third World is nothing but a drain on the First World nations and international lending institutions, it is important to point out that the Third World pays back more in debt repayment than it receives in aid from the First World. According to a World Bank report, the Third World repaid fifty-two billion dollars more in debt repayment than they received in aid from the First World.[3]

Foreign assistance to Third World countries is claiming more attention today than it ever has for a number of reasons. First, the Third World's debt has reached astronomical proportions in just the last decade and a half; it now stands at 1.3 trillion dollars. Second, several Third World countries have threatened to default on their loans or withhold payment on principal or interest. Finally, there is serious question as to whether the Third World will ever be in a position to repay its debt in full. As a student of mine said, "What are we going to do, go into Mexico and confiscate all of their TVs, cars, radios, and refrigerators?" He was not all that far from the truth.

While we have not confiscated the TVs, cars, radios, and refrigerators of the Third World, in point of fact we are confiscating the food, housing, medical care, and education of the poor. The rich have ways of protecting their wealth; the poor have none. It is the poor, particularly the children of the poor, who are paying back the Third World's debt with their lives.

Since the colonial era, the economies of Third World nations have been oriented toward the export of primary products and raw minerals to the First World. To make matters worse, their economies are dependent on the export of one or two primary products or minerals. To this day, half of all Third World nations continue to depend on the export of one or two cash crops or minerals for fifty percent of their export earnings. Africa is a prime example of this. Today, nine African nations derive seventy percent of their export earnings from just one cash crop.[4]

Because the bulk of its trade, almost eighty percent, is transacted with the First World, the Third World depends on the First World for access to its markets and a just price for its exports. Shrinking markets and prices prevent Third World nations from purchasing goods and services they desperately need to sustain and develop their economies.

The nations of the Third World have argued that, over the last three decades, their exports have met increased protectionism from the First World. This has been the case particularly for processed goods (which command higher prices on the world market and generate greater profit). In addition, they have experienced a significant decrease in their export earnings, compared with a steady increase in the cost of goods and services they must import from the First World. In the first half of the 1980s, for example, the price of Third World raw materials and minerals fell by eighteen percent. This breaks down to a loss in income of forty billion dollars per year—more than all the aid the Third World received during that period.[5] In short, the nations of the Third World find themselves in the unenviable position of having to produce more and more to purchase less.

To compensate for the difference between export earnings and import costs, the Third World must resort to borrowing and begging. Aid can come from a number of sources. The Third World can borrow from First World governments, from multilateral institutions, like the International Monetary Fund and the World Bank Group, and from commercial banks.

Until the early 1970s, the Third World was able to manage its debt. Then, all hell broke loose. By tracing the events that took place over the last two decades, I think it will become clear why I argue that hunger is related to poverty and debt. I hope it will also become clear why I believe hunger is a political, economic, and also a moral problem, demanding a moral, political, and economic response.

The year 1973 is a key year in this story. It was the year the OPEC nations raised the price of oil. In just one year's time, the price of oil quadrupled. The rich nations responded by cutting back industrial activity. This hurt the nations of the Third World in at least two ways: (1) fewer raw materials and minerals were imported by the First World, and (2) the price of First World exports rose dramatically. It should also be remembered that 1973 marked the beginning of the world food crisis. The price of wheat, for example, increased from sixty dollars per ton in the second quarter of 1972 to two hundred ten dollars per ton in the first quarter of 1974. Rice rose from one hundred thirty-two dollars per ton to five hundred seventy dollars per ton in the same period. The non-oil producing Third World countries were forced to double or triple their borrowing to keep their economies going at pre-1970 levels.

On the other hand, the OPEC nations had a different kind of problem—what to do with this new money. The largest portion of it found its way to foreign commercial banks. For the commercial banks, the biggest problem was what to do with the new petrol dollars. The answer came in the form of making new loans to the Third World who needed money now more than they ever did. Stories abound today of hard sell tactics that were used to push loans on Third World borrowers. The loans, for the most part, were short term loans, made at variable rates. Oil prices rose again in 1978. This second price rise pushed the world further into recession. Whenever money is tight, funding for Third World development stagnates. The Third World's trade deficit almost doubled between 1979 and 1981, from forty-five billion dollars to ninety billion dollars.[6] Again, the commercial banks lent heavily to the most indebted nations.

To try to counter the effects of the recession, the United States and Britain initiated monetarist policies which, in turn, caused a sharp rise in interest rates. The effects of these policies were felt most severely by the Third World governments that borrowed so heavily during this period. A one percent increase in interest rates, for example, automatically added $700 million to Mexico's annual debt. By 1982, the recession, the decline in exports, the rising costs of imports, and the escalation of interest rates forced Mexico to declare that it could not meet payment on its eighty billion dollar foreign debt. This was followed by threats from other Latin American countries, and, in 1985, Peru's President, Garcia Perez, declared that his country would limit its debt payment to ten percent of the value of its imports. In 1987, Brazil, one of the largest debtor nations, declared that it would stop payments on interest.

Faced with the possible collapse of some of their banks, the United States and Britain intervened, and, through a combination of emergency loans and debt rescheduling, more money was made available to the biggest debtors to pay back old loans. A key player in this rescue operation was, and continues to be, the International Monetary Fund.

The International Monetary Fund was founded at the end of the Second World War. One of its purposes was to provide short term loans to nations experiencing a temporary balance of payments crisis. These loans save nations from having to curtail imports or impose trade restrictions. Resources for the IMF come from member nations who are assessed a quota based on their wealth when they become a member. The larger their quota, the greater their vote. The United States controls the largest vote in the IMF.

To qualify for an IMF loan, nations must agree to what is called an adjustment program. This program is designed by the IMF, supposedly to restore economic stability to the borrowing nations. It is premised on the assumption that the borrowing nation is in economic difficulty because of government mismanagement. The borrower signs a letter of intent, and the IMF advances money in installments, making periodic assessment of the borrower's compliance with these conditions. It is important to point out the role that the IMF has played historically in the global lending network. Countries who are refused loans through the IMF or who fall short of meeting the IMF adjustment program are considered poor credit risks and can count on having their loan requests through other multilateral, government, and commercial banks refused. To the global lending network, the IMF serves as a guarantor of a country's economic stability.

If one examines the requirements of the IMF adjustment program, it becomes obvious that the IMF's preferred corrective for economic instability is to slash government spending and increase exports. Its measures include: slashing government spending on social programs, eliminating government subsidies on food, raising interest rates, raising taxes, freezing wages, devaluing currency, abolishing trade restrictions, dismantling controls over foreign currency exchange, and increasing exports.

There is an African proverb that says, "Give a rich man less food, and he becomes thin; give a poor man less food, and he dies." It should come as no surprise that it is the most vulnerable members of society, those who are weakest and poorest, who pay the greatest price for the IMF adjustment program. The British journalist, Paul Vallely, points out that it is actually the children of the poor who are paying back the Third World's debt. However, they pay it back with their lives. Children, he argues, cannot ride out austerity programs; their mental and physical development takes place in the first five years of life. Without adequate nutrition and health care, they suffer permanent mental and physical impairment.[7]

While it is possible to demonstrate the effect of each of these measures on increasing hunger in the Third World, I would like to concentrate on one measure that is less obvious, but, in my judgment, more pernicious over the long run. I would argue that the IMF's requirement that the debtor nation strengthen its export sector, particularly its export of cash crops, not only cannot be justified, but is doing more to insure that the Third World never be in a position to feed itself.

At first glance, the IMF's insistence on strengthening the debtor nation's traditional export sector makes good sense for a number of reasons. Since the colonial period, trade in raw materials and minerals has been the primary source for generating foreign exchange. It prevents debtor nations from withdrawing from world trade and keeps exports flowing to where they have

always gone, the First World. It provides added incentive to
Third World and foreign governments, banks, and businesses
to develop further Third World natural resources. And, it can
increase a nation's Gross National Product.

All of that said, today the question is being raised as to
whether this approach to debt repayment does not, in fact, continue the legacy of colonialism which orients the Third World
toward the First World. Does it, in fact, represent a form of
development or anti-development? Finally, what effect does
stimulating the export sector, especially cash crops, have on the
land tenure system, the distribution of wealth, the destruction
of the environment, and the ability of poor nations to feed
themselves?

When debtor nations are pressured by the IMF to increase
their traditional export sector, a number of things happen. It is
important not to lose sight of the fact that a number of Third
World nations export the same products: sugar, coffee, ba-
nanas, beef, et cetera. When they individually increase their
export volume, they also increase competition among themselves. Competition, in turn, drives the prices for the exports
down. While lower prices benefit First World nations, the Third
World cannot afford them.

For them to stay competitive, that is, to earn the foreign exchange to pay their debt, something must give. And, it is usually labor. Either farming becomes more mechanized,
displacing landless laborers, or salaries are further reduced. In
either case, the poor who work the farms become even poorer
and hungrier.

When a debtor nation's exports are primarily cash crops,
there is added incentive for governments themselves, or governments in cooperation with the wealthy, to buy up the more pro-
ductive land or use whatever means necessary, including
violence, to push subsistence farmers off that land. This exacer-
bates an already serious land tenure problem in many Third
World nations. Again, it is the poor who lose out. What little
economic and political power their land may have afforded
them is now taken away. What is more, it is justified in the
name of repaying the national debt. Unemployment and hunger increase among subsistence farmers, and the poor themselves, who depended on food from those farmers, grow hungrier.
Land that was once used for growing food for local consumption
is now used to grow cash crops — crops for export. Where corn,
beans, melons, squash once grew, today cash crops, like soya
peanuts, cassava, now grow, or cattle graze — all making their
way into the bellies of the First World.

A 1982 United Nations' study maintained that all but four Sahelian nations have the capacity to feed themselves.[8] In fact, until 1970, Africa was growing enough food to feed itself.[9] In 1984, the year of the famine, record harvests of 154 million tons of cotton were exported from Senegal, Mali, Burkina Faso, Niger, and Chad. However, it should also be noted that during that period the price of cotton on the international market steadily fell.[10] Land that can grow cotton in a drought can just as easily grow food.

To survive, peasants are forced to farm more marginal land or the fragile soil of tropical rain forests. The traditional methods of restoring nutrients to the land through crop rotation or by allowing the land to lie fallow for a period of time are impossible, given the scarcity of good land and the burden of overpopulation. Consequently, more and more of the land and forests in the Third World are lost each year because of overcultivation, overgrazing, and deforestation. The result is human and ecological devastation. Hunger, poverty, and the ecological crisis, far from being separate, are, in fact, related issues. The famous United Nations Commission report on the environment, *Our Common Future*, goes so far as to say that "the reduction of poverty itself is a precondition for environmentally sound development."[11]

This IMF measure contributes toward hunger in yet another way. It encourages Third World and foreign banks, corporations, and development agencies to invest heavily in the cash crop sector. Consequently, more advice, government credit, research and development agency investment are made available for cash cropping instead of for growing food to feed a poor and hungry population.

With less food available for local consumption, the price of food escalates dramatically. Brazil is a good illustration of this point. Brazil is one of the most heavily indebted nations of Latin America. It is also the second largest exporter of agricultural commodities in the world. Yet, half of its population is undernourished. Over the last two decades, encouraged by the IMF, Brazil increased its soya acreage by twenty percent. (Its soya, incidentally, is shipped to the First World to feed livestock.) During that same period of time, the price of black beans, the food staple of the local population, rose by 275 percent.[12]

Finally, there is every incentive for Third World farmers to grow cash crops instead of food crops. In many cases, Third World governments, forced to comply with the IMF program, will themselves purchase, store, and market the cash crops, thus relieving farmers of the usual uncertainties that go with farming.

Sociologists Ralph Sell and Steven Kunitz examined the relationship between debt and life expectancy. Using the most reliable data they could find from seventy-three African, Asian, and Latin American countries between 1970-80, they found that the more heavily indebted a country, the lower the life expectancy: "Each additional $10 a year in interest payments (per capita) reflected 0.39 of a year less in life expectancy improvement over the decade (1970-80)."[13] According to Susan George's calculations, this works out to an average of 387 days of life lost for every man, woman, and child in those seventy-three countries.[14]

It is no accident that the IMF chooses the measure described above to insure repayment of the Third World's debt. These policies are determined by its more powerful member nations, particularly the United States. The fact that hunger and death should increase is of little concern as long as the interest to foreign creditors continues to be repaid. While it is doubtful that anyone in the United States, Europe, or Japan would suffer significantly or die if the Third World's debt or the terms of repayment were restructured, it is certain that it is the poor in the Third World who are bearing the heaviest cost of repayment. The poor are sacrificed on the altar of the world banking system.

The IMF claims that it is not a development agency and that that particular job is best left to its sister institution, the World Bank. However, as I have pointed out above, its policies determine the type of development that takes place in Third World debtor nations. Moreover, because of its influence on other banks, development agencies, governments, and corporations, it plays no small role in determining the needs that are met and unmet, and the concerns that are and are not addressed in the Third World.

There are numerous studies that severely criticize the type of development the IMF policies promote. They maintain that economic, political, and social inequality in Third World nations must be addressed if serious and long term development is ever to take place. Policies that foster land redistribution, self reliance, and that promote the integration and participation of the majority of the poor in the economic and political life of Third World societies are the only hope for solving the Third World's poverty and hunger. Today, we are more convinced than we ever were that a solution to world hunger lies, not with food aid, food imports, or large scale corporate farming, but with subsistence farmers and locally directed sustainable, spreadable community projects.

There is no reason that IMF policies cannot promote social equality rather than inequality. There is no reason it cannot support subsistence farmers over corporate farmers. There is no reason it cannot favor the integration and participation of the poor in the economic and political structure of debtor nations. And, there is no reason its influence cannot be used to encourage governments to promote food self reliance. Yet, the IMF would prefer to ignore the needs of the poor and hungry and provide yet another justification to exploit them. In short, for the IMF to continue its approach to debt repayment suggests disdain for the poor and a total disregard for human suffering, life, and ecological destruction.

I never tire of telling my students that there are many ways to kill. While we prefer to think that only criminals kill using bullets, and governments kill during war using missiles, the lives of millions of human beings in the Third World, particularly children and the elderly, are killed through the economic policies of banks. Banks do it quite legitimately and effectively with our money and in our name. But, neither they nor we are used to thinking of what they do in terms of killing. In Susan George's words, "The managers are not trained to entertain the notion that their activities might have anything to do with such embarrassing categories as life and death."[14] Whether it is by using bullets or by withholding bread, people die just the same.

Now, back to our original question: how to feed the hungry today, given the causes of hunger analyzed above?

I believe that the Church can play a significant role in ending global poverty and hunger. But, it remains to be seen as to whether it will assume that role. As I see it, this depends to a large extent on whether the Church is willing to venture into unfamiliar territory — on whether it can extricate itself from its present preoccupation with the private and interpersonal dimensions of human existence and preach and witness to the Gospel in more public and political ways. In short, it is dependent upon whether the Church can come to terms with the fact that the public and political today are the arenas of its ministry.

Before going further, let me define my use of the terms public and political. Public is the opposite of the private. It is that area of human existence that can be seen by others, shared by others, and is open to scrutiny. Political refers to the ordering or structuring of the public. It refers to the institutions, the forum, and the process that govern or regulate the affairs of the public.

If the Church is committed to feeding the hungry in this day and age, then it must be willing to address, not only the private or interpersonal dimensions of our lives, but the public and political as well. The starting point for reflecting on our responsibility as people of faith to end poverty and hunger must be a recognition of the fact that we are linked to one another and, consequently, bound to one another through the public and political institutions of our global society. Our lives are not only private nor are our relationships solely interpersonal. We are economic and political beings. In fact, were we to examine the greater part of the day of most adults, it would become clear that the bulk of our time and activity and the majority of our relationships are economic and political. Our relationship with the poor and hungry in the United States and throughout the world, for example, is not interpersonal, but economic and political. We rarely see the faces of the poor and hungry and do not know their names. Nevertheless, we are in relationship with them through institutional arrangements of which we are a part, through what we consume, through loans, through investments, through corporations, and through our government's foreign and domestic policy.

These institutional relationships, while neither recognized by us nor significant to us, are most certainly recognized and experienced by the poor and hungry of the world. As we pointed out above, economic and political institutions can cause grave human misery and death. Because these relationships destroy life and dignity and also have the potential to further and enhance life and dignity, they are not neutral, even though we would prefer to think of them as such. They, as all relationships, are under the judgment of God. Thus, it seems that the institutional Church cannot ignore our economic and political relationships with the poor in our global society. It must find ways to address the Gospel to us in precisely those relationships.

While the Church's social teaching emphasizes that we are fundamentally social beings, it too easily falls into the trap of reducing social to interpersonal. Consequently, the command to love the neighbor is reduced to loving only those with whom we enter into interpersonal relationships. If it is true that our relationships with the poor and hungry are economic and political and we are linked to them through the structural and systemic arrangements, then the Church can ignore those relationships only at the great price of increasing suffering and death.

In the 1940s, the German theologian, Dietrich Bonhoeffer, reflecting on the indifference on the part of the Christian com-

munity to the gassing of Jews, criticized the Church for allowing God to be pushed out of the center of life and squeezed into
the most private and most intimate realms of our existence. He
argued that pastors seemed to take delight in meddling in those
most delicate and sensitive areas of human existence. Pastors
seemed to prey on their congregations where they were most
vulnerable. The private, the sexual, for example, had come to
be the only area left to the Church. When the time came for the
Church to address the community of faith in the areas of their
public and political responsibilities, it was not equipped to do so
precisely because it had relinquished those areas to the State.
From my own observations, the Church has not changed much
from the time of Bonhoeffer. It has not learned from the experience of the Holocaust, from Vietnam, Cambodia, or from the
war in the Persian Gulf.

Besides taking seriously our economic and political relationships, the Church needs to take seriously the institutions themselves and the process of institutional change. The Church
seems to operate on the naive assumption that good people, got-
ten into high places, can transform institutional structures and
systems. If matters of economic and political justice are addressed at all from the pulpit or in the classroom, the message
concentrates on personal conversion. The assumption is that, if
individuals are converted to the poor and their struggle for justice, those individuals will automatically effect social change.
Good people make institutions good. While it would be foolish
to minimize the good that one person can do, the fact of the
matter is that institutions cannot be reduced to the people who
work within them. They are more than people. They have their
own history, their own agenda, their own goals and objectives,
and their own value system. Their agenda, goals, objectives,
and values are embedded in their very function and structure.
Thus, for the Church to concentrate only or primarily on
changing the minds and hearts of individuals within institutions
without also addressing the necessity of restructuring economic
and political structures and systems is for the Church to fall
short of its responsibility.

If God is indeed Lord of all creation, God is Lord of all economic and political structures and systems. They are subject to
God's judgment and redemption. In sum, the Church must address us regarding our mutual moral responsibility for our economic and political relationships within institutions and for the
institutions themselves. The Church must contribute to the
conversion of individuals and to the conversion of structures.

Let me say a word here on the conversion of structures. As I mentioned above, it is not simply a matter of changing the minds and hearts of individuals. Rarely do economic and political structures and systems change by using moral persuasion alone. Conflict, confrontation, coercion, and the use of power must inevitably be employed. The Church's attitude toward the above is to avoid them, lament them, or point out their dangers.[15] I believe the Church must come to terms with the fact that a number of economic and political policies and practices conflict with everything the Christian tradition represents. They must be confronted, and means, in addition to moral persuasion, must be used to effect change. John Coleman argues the need for a Christian theory of citizenship.[16] I can think of no better place for the Church to start.

If the poor and hungry are victims of institutions and their policies and if our relationship to the poor and hungry is not interpersonal, but public and political, then it seems that the Church must preach and witness to the Gospel in new ways—in ways that reveal the public and political character of Jesus and the reign of God.

There are many strains that run through the Gospels. It is easy to focus on Jesus' interpersonal relationships, or his love for his disciples, or his compassion for the handicapped, or his forgiveness for the sinner, or his miracles. To emphasize these, however, and ignore the public and political character of Jesus' life and teaching would be to rob the Gospel of the fullness of its truth and its possibility of speaking to us in the complexity of our existence today. Given the public and political nature of poverty and hunger, the Church must resist the temptation to emphasize the private and interpersonal at the expense of the public and political.

The German political theologians, I believe, are correct in arguing that the Gospels are not a biography of a private individual. Rather, they are a summons to live and to structure our existence in new ways. They are a summons to live the truth in more public and political ways.

Jesus was not only a private individual, but he was very much a public and a political figure. And, his message was very much a public and a political message. The Gospels tell us that Jesus was not one for keeping to himself. They tell us that he went around preaching publicly to all who would hear. He was known in the towns he visited, and he drew crowds. Sometimes, the crowds sat at his feet, and at times they grew restless and unruly and tried to run him out of town. One thing we are sure of is that he was not uncontroversial. Moreover, the truth he spoke gave the religious and political authorities of his day cause for alarm. He so disturbed them and the truth he spoke so threatened the social order that they had to have him arrested, tortured, publicly tried, and publicly executed. He died the death of a political criminal.

The truth that Jesus spoke and witnessed to was not "be nice to one another or be neighborly," as it is so often preached in our churches. It was the truth of the impending reign of God. God's reign was marked by love, justice, peace. Jesus preached a reversal of the old order: the hungry were to be fed, the naked clothed, the homeless sheltered, and the thirsty given drink. The first were to be last and the last, first. Jesus invited his disciples to participate in this reign and to further it.

Just as the Church must resist the tendency to reduce the Gospels to a biography of a private individual, it must also resist the temptation to reduce the truth that Jesus spoke and acceptance of that truth to interior attitudes. While love, peace, justice are indeed attitudes, they are never merely that. They are also public and political realities. Peace, for example, as Pope Paul VI reminded us in his encyclical, *On the Development of Peoples*, is something which is built day in and day out. It has to do with establishing just relationships — not only interpersonal relationships, but institutional relationships — just economic and political structures and systems within nations and among nations.

Can love, in the ideal, in the abstract, or in general, be called love at all? Our very understanding of these realities is always grounded in concrete human experience. Human beings can hope only for specific things, love specific people, struggle for specific ends. Love, peace, justice, and hope, in the mind or in the abstract or in the ideal, are not the realities love, peace, and justice. If the reign of God is not the idea of love, peace, and justice, but the reality expressed in concrete terms, then to accept the truth of God's reign is to accept nothing less than love, justice, and peace in our economic and political institutions and systems.

A favorite author of mine, Ronald Marstin, has written: "While the idea of justice may involve a change of consciousness, the reality will involve a change of society. . . It will matter little if, as the mind grows, the vision expands, the social structure itself remains unchanged."[17] The Church cannot continue to preach faith only as an interior attitude or disposition. Jesus preached that the way to know God, to love God, was not through what we say, but through what we do. The Gospels tell us that the way to know and love God is through loving the neighbor, particularly the weakest members of society. The Church must remind us time and time again that our neighbors are the masses of humanity who are oppressed, social classes, nations, races, and women. If our relationship to them is economic and political, then love will have to take on economic and political forms. In sum, to accept the truth of God's reign is to accept it, not only regarding our minds and hearts, but also regarding the economic and political institutions of our global society. To accept the truth of God's reign is to accept it by acting in a way that furthers it in the economic and political institutions of society. Thus, faith is a public and political act. It does not accept the unjust economic and political relationship or structural arrangements as final, but struggles to change them.

As mentioned above, if the Church is to play a role in ending poverty and hunger, it must not only preach in ways that are more public and political, but it must also witness in ways that are more public and political. The Church is an institution that is both public and political. It is public in that its buildings, resources, personnel, its statements and actions represent something in society. Since Jesus was a public figure and spoke his truth publicly and addressed it to the public institutions of his day, the Church, which is charged with the responsibility of transmitting the Gospel, must preach it publicly. It is also political in that it influences society. What it addresses and does not address, the way it acts and does not act, what it supports and does not support, influence the organization or structure of society. It influences the distribution of wealth and power. The Church acts as a force that maintains the order of the global society or challenges it. It influences society by what it chooses to do and not do.

Walter Brueggemann, in a wonderful essay, suggests that the Church indeed has a public and political role to play and is being unfaithful to its mission if it fails to assume it.[18] Brueggemann, drawing on the story of the Israelites' struggle for liberation, argues that what they had and what we as a people of faith have to offer society are alternative perceptions of public and political reality. He argues that Israel's story is one of "sacred discontent." Because of its belief in Yahweh and Yahweh's promises, Israel knew that the dominant interpretation of reality was not absolute. Nor was it the only interpretation there was. Consequently, it refused to accept it. Israel knew that the dominant interpretation of reality was structured by the Empire for its own interests. The story of Israel is the story of a people who, because of their experience of suffering and hope in God's promises, chose to expose the falseness of that interpretation of reality and to bring to light the truth of human suffering.

It was the hope of the Egyptians that injustice of society would go unnoticed or, if noticed, be accepted as necessary to the affairs of State. They counted on the dominant interpretation of reality being accepted as the only interpretation there was. It was the hope of the Egyptians that the truth of human suffering would not be known. But, the story of Israel is the story of a people who brought pain and suffering to public expression and who refused to accept it as reality because they believed in another reality.

Thus, it seems that, if the Church is to play a role in ending poverty and hunger, it cannot accept the starvation of a billion people as normal, necessary, or inevitable. Nor can it be indifferent to economic and political institutions and policies that would sacrifice human life to repay debt. If it is faithful to the Judeo-Christian tradition, it must bring this reality — the true cost of policies measured in terms of human suffering — over and over again to public expression. It must never let the State forget that this level of human suffering is real and that it is intolerable. It seems that it must do everything in its power to destabilize the rationale or the justifications for this suffering — the rationale that would lull us into believing that it is normal, necessary, or acceptable. In addition, it must do everything in its power to take those explanations that would remove us from responsibility for the suffering and expose their falseness.

The power of speaking the truth and using the Church's influence to further the truth was brought home to me in the murder of the six Salvadoran Jesuits in November of 1989. To speak the truth in a society that does not want to hear it and to speak it in places where it is never heard, in public and political forums, are dangerous things to do. What struck me about the Jesuits was that they refused to ignore the suffering and death in their society. They used the public vehicles available to them, the pulpit, the press, the media, the classroom, university offices, symposia, and conferences. They used their public status to further the truth. And, for that they paid a great price. The empire dealt with them much the way it did with Jesus. The truth is so strong, so threatening to the Establishment, that it had to be destroyed.

So, the Church must be a public witness to the suffering of two thirds of humanity. But, it cannot merely bemoan such massive suffering as it has in the past. It must go a step further. It must dare to expose publicly the specific policies and practices that rob people of food, that kill, and dehumanize. It needs to do this in the pulpit and in public.

If the Church is committed to not only interpreting the world, but to transforming it, to not only speaking the truth, but furthering it, then it must engage in public and political action. Richard McBrien argues that the Church has the right and, indeed, the duty to enter public policy debate and to shape public policy when matters of human rights, peace and justice, or salvation are involved.[19] Thus, it seems to me that, if the Church is going to play a role in ending global poverty and hunger, it must witness to the Gospel publicly by engaging in public policy debates. It is its responsibility to raise the moral issues in public policy debates, facilitate the engagement of its members in these issues, and shape these issues through lobbying and public action.

Let me say a few words about the Church's involvement in politics. It is my judgment that the religious and the political have much more in common than we care to admit. I would argue further that to engage in shaping public policy opens the Church to the possibility of knowing the truth of the Gospel more fully, of living it more faithfully, and of furthering it. It likewise holds true that, to refuse to engage in the political, the Church runs the risk of not knowing, living, and furthering. "Permanence and universality in the realm of truth and value," Charles Davis argues, "are desired achievements; they cannot be prior claims."[20] What Davis is saying here is that the truth is not something to be had once and for all by either an institution or individuals. It is the nature of truth to be alive, to be constantly unfolding. It is only by living the truth that the truth actually becomes truth for us. It is only in practice that we come to know the truth. Truth is such that it unfolds in the process of living it. As we live it, our understanding of it is stretched. In addition, it is only in living the truth that we are claimed by it and thus can speak of its claim on us. This living and speaking lead us to live further into the truth. It is my judgment that, by refusing to speak about the public and political from the pulpit, by refusing to speak the truth about human suffering in public and to engage in public and political debate and action, the Church admits that the public and political are devoid of truth. But, more importantly, in cutting the public and political off, the Church cuts itself off from living and understanding the truth more fully.

The political is not foreign to the religious. It is an arena in which truth is spoken, is chosen, is lived, and is furthered and tested. It is an arena in which something new is generated and community is formed. It is, in short, an arena in which God's reign is furthered. If the Church must not simply speak the truth of God's reign, but participate in extending it, then the political cannot be excluded from its preaching or witness.

I think it behooves the Church to look seriously at what the religious and the political hold in common. When we talk about the political, we are talking, not simply about strategies, but ideals. While the political is concerned with present reality, it is just as much concerned with the future of that reality. It is a sphere in which we envision possibilities for the present, possibilities that may enhance the quality of life or detract from it.

Politics, at its best, tries to improve on what already is. It could be argued that restlessness or dissatisfaction is characteristic of the political. In other words, in the political arena, the present is not the final word, nor is it the ultimate truth. Change is part and parcel of the political. The present can always be improved upon. Theologians have called this need to envision, to go beyond what already is, and this restlessness within ourselves, transcendence. Thus, it would seem that, rather than trying eagerly to disengage itself from the political, the Church might look at the political in a new light. Perhaps the political is itself, not something totally secular or foreign to the religious, but an expression of our own transcendence.

What is being fought out or contested in the political arena is a vision of life. In John Coleman's words, "Politics represents the arena where the struggle between good and evil occurs in concrete terms around policies and legislation."[21] The decisions that are made are about priorities. The visions adopted in the political arena ultimately determine who lives and who dies. They also affect the quality of those lives. In short, the public policy has a major share in protecting and promoting life.

The political is also a means of embodying and testing the truth. The truth of our vision and our priorities is validated in our minds. The truth of our vision becomes real and tested only as it takes form and is lived. Undoubtedly, in embracing the political, in preaching and witnessing to the Gospel in more public and political ways, the Church takes risks. Its words and actions may be misunderstood. It may also have to bear contradiction and uncertainty. And, it can expect polarization. But, perhaps polarization is not the greatest threat to the Church.[22]

Perhaps in saving its life, by focusing on the familiar, the private and interpersonal, the Church has been losing its life and with it the lives of a billion people. In daring to lose its life, in daring to preach and witness to the truth publicly and politically, it may yet find it.

NOTES

[1]Lloyd Timberlake, *Africa in Crisis: The Causes, the Cures of Environmental Bankruptcy* (Philadelphia: New Society Publishers, 1986), 15-16.
[2]Paul Vallely, *Bad Samaritans: First World Ethics and Third World Debt* (Maryknoll, N.Y.: Orbis Books, 1990), 80.
[3]Ibid., 4.
[4]Ibid., 105-6.
[5]Ibid., 106.
[6]Susan George, *A Fate Worse Than Debt: The World Financial Crisis and the Poor* (New York: Grove Press, 1988), 48.
[7]Vallely, 9.
[8]Timberlake, 38.
[9]Ibid., 71.
[10]Vallely, 50.
[11]World Commission on Environment and Development, *Our Common Future* (New York: Oxford University Press, 1987), 69.
[12]Vallely, 113.
[13]George, 134.
[14]Ibid., 6.
[15]John A. Coleman, "The Two Pedagogies: Discipleship and Citizenship," in *Education for Citizenship and Discipleship*, ed. Mary C. Boys (New York: The Pilgrim Press, 1989), 45.
[16]Ibid., 43.
[17]Ronald Marstin, *Beyond Our Tribal Gods: The Maturing of Faith* (Maryknoll, N.Y.: Orbis Books, 1979), 51.
[18]Walter Brueggemann, "The Legitimacy of a Sectarian Hermeneutic: 2 Kings 18-19," in *Education for Citizenship and Discipleship*, ed. Mary C. Boys (New York: The Pilgrim Press, 1989), 3-34.
[19]Richard P. McBrien, *Caesar's Coin: Religion and Politics in America* (New York: Macmillan Publishing Company, 1987), 19.
[20]Charles Davis, *Theology and Political Society* (Cambridge: Cambridge University Press, 1980), 26.
[21]Coleman, 56.
[22]Edward Schillebeeckx, *On Christian Faith: The Spiritual, Ethical and Political Dimensions* (New York: Crossroad, 1987), 83.

The Works of Mercy: Housing the Homeless

Peter R. Gathje

I. Introduction: The Works of Mercy and Homelessness

Ministry with the homeless inevitably involves the works of mercy, both corporal and spiritual. Traditionally, mercy has been understood as resulting from charity; God's love for us enables us to love our neighbor. In charity, when we love our neighbors, we come to grieve over their sorrows as if they were our own. Mercy combines this solidarity in suffering and sorrow with the will to transform the situation and alleviate the suffering. As such, solidarity with the homeless poor and efforts to address their suffering are contemporary forms of mercy.

The traditional lists of both the corporal and spiritual works of mercy are solidly grounded in Scripture. Two passages have been central for the development of the corporal works of mercy. The first, Isaiah 58:6-7, states:

> Is not this the fast that I choose: to loose the bonds of wickedness, to undo the thongs of the yoke, to let the oppressed go free, and to break every yoke? Is it not to share your bread with the hungry and bring the homeless poor into your house?

It is important to note that this Isaiah passage is part of a larger prophetic message found throughout Isaiah and other prophets in the Hebrew Scriptures. The prophets stress that concrete acts of mercy for the neighbor are a prerequisite for the proper worship of God. Love of God and love of neighbor are inseparable.[1]

This theme continues in the New Testament passage that is central to the tradition of the corporal works of mercy. In Matthew 25:31-46, Jesus describes the Last Judgment. He tells us that we will be judged by the way we feed the hungry, give drink to the thirsty, welcome the stranger, clothe the naked, and visit the sick and imprisoned. We meet the Son of Man in those

93

who are in need and are on the margins of society. True love of
God is necessarily expressed in mercy for the suffering neighbor. Thus, in 1 John 3:17, we read, "He who has the goods of
this world and sees his brother in need and closes his heart to
him, how does the love of God abide in him?"

A variety of Scriptural texts have been cited with regard to
the spiritual works of mercy.[2] In contrast to the corporal works
of mercy, these passages focus on the way the spiritual works of
mercy attend to the interpersonal aspects of human existence.
Such works are especially concerned with the character of one's
relationships to God and other persons. This does not imply a
separation of the two types of works of mercy. Rather, the spiritual and corporal works of mercy must be held together since
mercy is concerned with the whole person, spirit and body. To
ignore bodily needs when ministering to the spiritual denies our
embodied nature as human beings. Offering corporal works of
mercy without the spiritual can easily lead to depersonalization.
Mercy, grounded in God's undeserved love, creates relationships of mutuality and equality. True mercy does not deny common physical needs, neither does it treat others as objects.

Keeping these basic themes in mind, I want to consider first
what form this mercy should take with regard to the homeless. I
will then describe an intentional Christian community's attempts to engage in the works of mercy with the homeless, the
Open Door Community of Atlanta, Georgia.[3] I will close with
some reflections on what we might learn about the works of
mercy from this community and its ministry with the homeless.

II. Homelessness in the United States:
Mercy and Membership

It was in the late 1970s that the homeless populations in major cities began to garner attention in the media. In time, the
stereotype of homeless persons as older men, troubled by alcohol abuse, who lived on "Skid Row" began to be shaken by the
realities of a new kind of homelessness. Women and children,
along with younger men, were increasingly seen on the streets.
Further, the homeless were becoming more visible throughout
downtown areas, sleeping on heating grates or in train stations,
panhandling shoppers and business people, and lining up for
soup kitchens opening at downtown churches. The numbers of
homeless in the United States appeared to be growing again
after a period of decline in the 1950s and 1960s.

The exact number of homeless today remains notoriously difficult to ascertain.[4] Different definitions of what it means to be

homeless, different methods of counting, and the politics of the issue have all served to produce widely varying estimates of the number of homeless persons. They range from the controversially low estimate of 350,000 homeless, offered in a HUD study in 1986, to the estimates of advocacy groups for the homeless which find close to three million persons on the streets.[5] In Atlanta, estimates of the number of homeless range from 3,000 to 15,000 people. These statistical disputes are but one indicator that the presence of the homeless in cities of the United States is causing a public stir. Throughout the 1980s and continuing now into the 1990s, the issue of homelessness remains in the public eye, largely because homeless persons remain visible in almost every major city in the United States.

Who are the homeless? Peter Rossi notes that, contrary to current stereotypes of the homeless as mentally ill, drug and alcohol abusers, or physically incapable of work, studies of homeless persons reveal that "two-thirds of the homeless are not mentally ill, three-fifths are not alcoholics, three-fifths do not suffer disabling physical disorders, and 90 percent do not abuse drugs."[6] This is not to say that these are non-factors in homelessness. It is to suggest that homelessness is more adequately explained by looking at structural reasons for homelessness. One can certainly include among those structural factors the lack of residential care facilities for the homeless mentally ill who were de-institutionalized, and the lack of treatment for substance abusers among the poor due to the scarcity of rehabilitation centers. Yet, these ills and society's insufficient response to them certainly do not account for the numbers of homeless.

A more accurate understanding of homelessness begins with viewing it as the tip of a giant iceberg of poverty in our society. Approximately thirty-five million people fall below the official poverty line in terms of income. From among these poor, those who end up on the streets do so for a variety of reasons. Generally, it is a financial or personal crisis that strains already thin resources that leads to life on the streets.

What structural factors precipitate this fall into homelessness? Michael Walzer's concept of "membership" provides a useful framework for analyzing both the structural reasons for homelessness and the situation of homeless persons. Walzer describes membership as that which determines who counts in a society and who participates in the decisions shaping social life.[7] Non-members are excluded from participation in society. This exclusion blocks them from the communal provision of goods and from the protections society offers in the marketplace and elsewhere.

It is relatively easy to establish parallels between the situation
of the homeless and what Walzer describes as the situation of
non-members. Two important structural factors in the rise of
homelessness indicate the way homeless persons have become
non-members in our society. The first refers to the lack of communal provision in terms of housing. The second illustrates the
lack of protection offered the homeless in the marketplace.

The simplest answer to the question of why homelessness is
increasing in the United States is the lack of affordable housing.[8] In the 1980s, when the number of households at or below
the poverty level increased by thirty-six percent, the federal
government was either cutting back or holding at existing levels
its programs for low income housing. At the same time, the
change from a manufacturing to a service based economy was
adversely affecting earnings, making housing more unafforda-
ble.[9]

The lack of affordable housing has been exacerbated by the
destruction of Single Room Occupancy (SRO) hotels. SROs
traditionally served as the housing of last resort for the most
marginalized of the poor. These have been systematically destroyed in major cities due to urban renewal projects consisting
largely of office and hotel developments. In Atlanta, for example, a study revealed that almost ninety percent of SRO housing
was destroyed during the 1970s and 1980s. Nationally, the destruction extended to some fifty-five percent of SRO housing.[10]
As a result, persons already on the edges of the housing market
find themselves unable to procure housing. With an estimated
6.3 million Americans paying more than fifty percent of their
income for rent, it should come as no surprise that some of these
people end up on the streets.

The second factor in the rise of homelessness emerges from
changes in the economy that impact on the labor market. Technological changes and the transition to a service economy have
caused a dramatic decline in the number of jobs available to the
unskilled and undereducated. Typically, these people had found
employment in jobs related to manufacture. At the same time,
the postwar baby boom led to an increased number of young
people seeking such work. This has further intensified the competition for these jobs. Consequently, frequent unemployment
and decreased earnings increasingly haunt those with low skills,
making them ever more susceptible to homelessness. This poor
labor market is especially hard on those already vulnerable in
the economy: racial minorities, women, and the physically or
mentally disabled. Sporadic employment in low-paying jobs,

coupled with the loss of low-income housing, forces many people onto the streets.

Those who become marginalized in the job market in this way find that labor pools become their usual place of employment. As homelessness increased in the 1980s, temporary employment services became one of the fastest growing industries in the United States.[11] These labor pools primarily hire homeless persons to engage in difficult and dangerous work on behalf of companies in need of such temporary help. The pools charge the companies ten dollars or more an hour, while paying the actual laborers near minimum wage. The laborers are not covered by workers' compensation or unemployment insurance. That the homeless function in our economy to provide this type of temporary and hard labor is further evidence of their status as non-members. As Walzer observes, historically non-members have functioned in a society "to free the citizens (members) from hard and unpleasant work."[12]

Behind this analysis of the structural causes of homelessness are the homeless themselves. Walzer describes the situation of non-members as harsh and life-threatening. Denied the goods necessary for decent human existence, non-members struggle for survival in a hostile environment. To be homeless is certainly to lack shelter, but it is also to lack resources for food, clothing, and medical care. Homeless people suffer from malnutrition; they endure a variety of physical ills, including tuberculosis, and they die from exposure.[13] But, homeless people also suffer from the social disdain and disapprobation given non-members. They represent failure in a society that worships success. They remind those who have succeeded that in our competitive society there is always the possibility of being left behind. And, finally, they (like the poor generally) often serve as societal scapegoats. They are a social blight, easily blamed for crimes, for the decline of downtown areas, and for the desecration of parks.

Ed Loring, of the Open Door Community, sketches a devastating portrait of homelessness as a situation of social exclusion and non-membership:

> Homelessness is absurd. Homelessness is unnecessary. Homelessness is hell. . . . Homelessness is dereliction, frostbitten toes, crooked and lost fingers. . . . What do you do when you have nothing to do? Something? Then you know little of the spiritual and political plight of the homeless boys and girls, women and men who roam downtown Atlanta to the chagrin of Central Atlanta Progress and the horror of the Chamber of Commerce and the dread of the banker who just sold one more

risk-free bond for the development of Underground Atlanta. There doctors and lawyers and business people will soon be able to "do anything they want" and never have to see, touch, hear, smell or taste the slowly dying, hidden lives and bodies of the homeless. What we have learned in modern America is that to have the poor available and ready is a social good for the well-to-do. That is when we want them as a source for blood plasma and for medical research or the manufacture of medicines, and as bodies for teaching hospitals, and as an ever ready, large pool of cheap labor. However, to have them present in our lives as anything other than objects for our benefit is bad for business and a blight upon our pleasure.[14]

Such a description reveals not only the pathos of being homeless, but also its connection with the structural factors discussed above. Together, the personal situation of the homeless and their social context indicate some of the complexity of the problem of homelessness in the United States. Keeping a focus on the question of membership helps to sort out some of the crucial issues. Are the homeless members of our society, and, if so, what obligations does that membership entail? Further, who is responsible for meeting those obligations? The way people respond to such questions reveals much about what they think about the homeless and their situation.

To help analyze these responses, I would like to suggest that mercy implies a recognition of membership, even as it is more than membership. Within Christian belief and practice, mercy emerges from the acknowledgment of a shared human existence as created and redeemed by God. From a Christian perspective, there are no strangers; no one is to be excluded from communal participation and provision. According to Walzer's social theory, membership emerges from the realization of shared practices and meanings.[15] Those who are outside of those practices and meanings are strangers. We are obligated to care for strangers only insofar as such care is urgently needed, and it does not involve high costs or risks for us.[16] Recognition of membership means a society is obligated to provide certain goods for persons, protect them from harm, and include them in the decisions which shape common life. Mercy, therefore, stands in critical relation to membership, since it pushes for the inclusion of strangers into a society. Mercy urges a society to recognize as members those whom a society excludes.

But, what prevents this recognition? To answer that question from a Christian perspective, I think it is helpful to employ a traditional distinction made by moral theologians. Mercy is distinguished from "sensible distress."[17] Both arise from the moral discomfort or intuitive sense that something is wrong when one encounters another's suffering. But, only in mercy does this natural abhorrence become transformed into a sustained effort to alleviate that suffering. With regard to the homeless, there has been considerable discussion concerning how best to solve the "problem" of homelessness. But, how much of that discussion has been grounded in mercy? Translated into social theory, how much of that discussion has been grounded in a recognition of membership?

Again turning to moral theology, one can identify three causes of an unmerciful spirit: "(a) lack of charity towards one in misery; (b) pride or too much prosperity, which makes one feel that others suffer justly, or that one is above their condition; and (c) great misfortune or fears that have hardened one's disposition or made one self-centered."[18] Current examples of these forms of an "unmerciful spirit" are easily found in positions taken regarding the homeless. At the same time, these positions reveal cultural attitudes that work to prevent the recognition of the homeless as members within our society.

Businesses in the neighborhood of the Open Door have continually pressured city officials to use police powers to clear the homeless from this area. Complaints about the unsightliness of the homeless who gather for soup each day at the Community's front door have led to police harassment of those in the soup line. Such complaints appear to be motivated either by a pride in prosperity or by a hardened disposition rooted in fear. As one letter sent to the Open Door put it, the homeless are

> . . . an eyesore and a hindrance to the revitalization of the Ponce de Leon corridor and downtown Atlanta. Many feel that downtown Atlanta may die on the vine because of flight to the suburbs by residents and business alike. Your facility is believed to exacerbate the problem.

Exhibiting a similar "unmerciful spirit," both city and business leaders in Atlanta have consistently considered homelessness a public nuisance rather than a public responsibility. A study of the downtown, commissioned by these leaders, reported that public safety was a major concern with regard to the homeless. The study concluded:

> Perceived safety is very poor, primarily due to the proliferation of street people and homeless on the streets and in the parks. Public facilities such as the library are gathering places for these people. . . . Many people fear the homeless who sleep in public areas, panhandle, and sometimes have alcohol or drug problems or are mentally unstable (Central Area Study II, 1987:17).

The Study recommended that the city create a "safeguard zone" in which increased numbers of police would patrol and arrest those perceived to be a public threat. A recently passed ordinance accomplishes these goals. Such actions confirm the non-membership of the homeless. As Walzer writes, for non-members the power of the State is experienced "as a pervasive and frightening power that shapes their lives and regulates their every move — and never asks for their opinion."[19]

A response grounded in mercy would not focus on punishing the homeless for their plight, but would encourage efforts by the city and business leaders to find resources to provide for the housing and other needs of the homeless. Without mercy, the inclusion of the homeless as members remains a distant goal.

III. The Open Door Community:
A Merciful Response to the Homeless

The mercy the Open Door Community extends to the homeless stands in sharp contrast to the retributive approach practiced by the city. Even as Community members recognize the shortcomings of their own efforts, they clearly reject responses that simply blame the homeless for their suffering. In their struggle to directly meet the needs of the homeless and in their political activity, they seek to be sensitive to both the structural and personal factors which contribute to a person's living on the streets. The Open Door witness offers a model for the way persons and communities can respond to homelessness. They call others to become involved directly with homeless persons. In this way, their ministry and witness are deeply shaped by the corporal and spiritual works of mercy. Their spirituality informs their work and the structure of their community life. In turn, these concretely embody the works of mercy. These works are aimed at basic human needs, both physical and spiritual, which must be met if a community of persons is to be created and maintained. The Open Door seeks to create what has been denied to the homeless in our society: a community in which all can participate with dignity and equality, and so share in the good life sustained through common labor. In a word, the Open Door struggles in its works of mercy to foster the recognition of the homeless as members.

To illustrate their ministry in relation to the works of mercy, I will first look at the Community's actions regarding the crucial physical needs of the homeless. The corporal works of mercy address basic human needs for food, drink, clothing, shelter, health, and community. Meeting these needs is a sign of at least partial membership. Thus, the actions of the Open Door that respond to those needs also have an implicit political nature. They indicate needs not met by society. The Community makes this political point explicit in various forms of protest. Second, I will consider the spirituality and ethics that ground these actions. Finally, I will examine the life of the Community itself. How has the Open Door sought to structure its own life in order to create a community in which the homeless become members? The spiritual works of mercy will become more central to the discussion in these two latter sections.

The Open Door's ministry with the homeless affirms that Christians must not only practice mercy, but recognize their own need for mercy. Since the mercy of the Christian is based in the charity of God, the works of mercy aim at creating in human relationships the equality and mutuality implied in that charity. They aim at the renewal of God's intention for human life together, and consequently they seek the full participation by all in the good of common life. This insight grounds the work of the Open Door as they offer soup and showers, as they publicly protest the injustice of homelessness in our society, and as they structure their life in community with homeless persons. It also shapes their work with prisoners on death row, but here I will focus on their ministry with the homeless.

Like many who responded to homelessness in the early 1980s, the founders of the Open Door Community first sought to provide shelter for the growing numbers of homeless persons. In 1979 in Atlanta, there were no church shelters and no shelters run by the city. There were some places homeless people could stay, such as the Union Mission and the Salvation Army, but these limited the number of nights a person could stay and required chapel attendance.

Seeking a social ministry for Clifton Presbyterian Church, Ed Loring (the church's pastor), his wife Murphy Davis, and two friends from the congregation decided to open a night shelter. In this decision, they were deeply influenced by the example of Dorothy Day and the Catholic Worker Movement, along with Mitch Synder from the Community for Creative Nonviolence, who came and spoke to their church. This shelter at Clifton Presbyterian, which opened in November of 1979, was the first free place of hospitality in the city of Atlanta.

Soon, the numbers of the homeless seeking shelter at Clifton made it evident that more shelters were needed. The four who initiated the Clifton shelter started encouraging other churches to also open their doors to the homeless. Their advocacy began to have results as one church after another opened shelters. By the fall of 1982, some sixteen churches in Atlanta were offering shelter. At present, there are about eighty shelters operated by a variety of organizations, most of which are run by churches or synagogues. The city of Atlanta opened its first shelter in the winter of 1983, after several homeless people froze to death and advocates for the homeless demonstrated in front of city hall for several days. These city operated shelters typically open only for the winter months.

The Open Door Community, which began in December of 1981, grew out of the Clifton night shelter experience. While they offered shelter, Loring, Davis and the Johnsons began recognizing the limits of this work. They continued to press other churches to open shelters as necessary to meet the most immediate physical needs of the homeless. But, they saw two important limits in this work. First, a shelter was not a home. The necessity of providing shelters, they argued, should not obscure the reality that shelters were a sign of our society's failure to provide decent housing for all of its members. Second, shelters perpetuated the divisions between those who gave shelter and the homeless who sought it. It was difficult to develop friendships involving real mutuality in a shelter setting. There was very little in the way of shared life. Further, race and class differences remained as barriers.

Thus, these four persons decided to form a community in which a common life might be fostered with homeless persons through shared work and worship. In creating the Open Door, they hoped to have a community in which both persons from middle class backgrounds and from the streets could be renewed in their humanity and dignity. The community would address the physical and spiritual needs of the homeless. But, this same community would also be a place where middle class persons could live in solidarity with the homeless poor. Such persons would thus leave behind their cultural addictions to material wealth and consumption. In an early interview, Ed explained what they sought in forming this community:

> We take seriously the word "hospitality" and we are attempting to offer hospitality and not just shelter. Theologically, hospitality means to us trying to offer space where people are not just sheltered and fed, but also are given friendship. And the basis for that is God's friendship with us.[20]

Out of this merciful response to God's love the Open Door Community was born. With the help of the Atlanta Presbytery, an old apartment building, located at 910 Ponce de Leon, a busy street near downtown, was purchased. After much renovation and cleaning, and with the addition of several volunteers, the Community began a soup kitchen on December 25, 1981. Other needs of the homeless became evident as the Community began to share life with homeless persons. Periods of time spent out on the streets allowed Community members to experience more directly what it meant to be homeless. One clear need of the homeless was a place to shower and get a change of clothes. Thus, in the summer of 1982 the Open Door started offering this service. Reflecting upon Matthew 25, Community members saw this work in a light similar to the soup kitchen: both were places where Christ was met in the guise of the homeless. In this spirit, Ed Loring drew an analogy between baptism and the showers which he called "another Kingdom washing." He wrote that "washing like eating, is related to the deepest mysteries of our sacramental communion with God in Christ. Showers and soup, shirts and sandwiches are offered and received here everyday. So is Jesus Christ."[21] Loring's analogy reflects the connection between sacramental symbolism and the works of mercy. Both efficaciously embody in outward signs the interior spirit of love.

In recognizing the sacramental character of the corporal works of mercy, the Community also discerned the communal, and thus societal, membership implications of these works. One Community member observed,

> . . . while offering hot water, soap, and towels to our tired and dirty sisters and brothers cannot wash away the injustice of a world that forces them to line up at our door in the cold morning hours, it is an offering that we must continue to give. For in this simple work of mercy, we are not only seeking to make more economic fruit accessible to those who have been denied it; we are also seeking to know the vagrant Christ who is standing tired and dirty, in that same shower line.

It is important to note the Open Door Community's conviction that the works of mercy are themselves political acts, since such works indicate a rejection of a system that perpetuates injustice. In a moment, I will consider in more detail this connection between acts of mercy and actions for justice.

Community members spending time on the streets also quickly learned about labor pools and the work available to the homeless. To get this physically demanding minimum wage work, a person must rise early. Working all day, one misses the soup kitchens which open for lunch and supper. The food sold on the lunch trucks that come to work sites is expensive. Homeless persons thus face the dilemma of eating or working. The Open Door sought to meet this problem by offering a breakfast at Butler Street C.M.E. church located downtown near a number of labor pools. As a result, since January of 1983, a breakfast of eggs, coffee, orange slices, a vitamin, and the "Southern delicacy" of grits is served each morning to some two hundred people. The breakfast allows homeless persons to begin work with a full stomach.

Like the shower line and the soup kitchen, the Butler Street breakfast and the other works of the Community are seen by the Open Door as acts of mercy. All of these works of mercy started in response to the needs of the homeless. However, they also see these works as symbols of injustice in our society. The Open Door finds that these works point to areas of common life where structural changes are necessary to create a just society. A Community handbook states:

> The soup kitchen is also a sign of degradation, violence and injustice with which this nation is filled. Hunger is a political manifestation of an economic system which serves the rich and starves the poor. We must never be satisfied with feeding the hungry Christ. Our compassion for the poor must be channeled into analysis and action that struggles to change the political and economic systems which are the root of hunger in America.

Recognizing that the corporal works of mercy are necessary because basic human needs are not being met within our society, the Open Door connects their actions of mercy with the struggle for justice. In terms of the homeless, this means ongoing public efforts to press for their inclusion as members within our society. Murphy Davis writes:

> Our little crumbs of service are not enough. What the poor and downtrodden need is not our piecemeal charity but justice. Not that we will close the soup kitchen or shower line or shelters. . . . But this is not an answer. An answer would only come in the form of justice. Wholeness. Enough for all God's children. . . . We must struggle to find the way to embody/incarnate the misery of the poor in the public arena.[22]

Thus, in addition to its works of mercy, the Open Door has repeatedly engaged in public demonstrations to keep the suffering of the homeless in the public consciousness and to advocate for structural changes necessary to meet the needs of homeless people.

Like their other works, these actions emerge out of the Community's relationships with the homeless, fostered within the Open Door, in service, and during times on the streets. Consequently, the Open Door engages in issues that are first raised by the homeless themselves. This shaping of the agenda by the homeless is an important affirmation of membership. The Community's actions reflect the concerns of the homeless and seek to extend this recognition of membership into society as a whole. Two examples illustrate this pattern.

The Open Door first learned of the need for public restrooms in the city of Atlanta from their friends on the streets. More than one hundred homeless people were being arrested every month on the charge of public urination, yet the city refused to provide public restrooms. In late 1983, the Community gained a public hearing on the issue from the Atlanta City Council. There, they urged city officials at least to put portable toilets in city parks. Dan Sweat, then the president of Central Atlanta Progress, an association of downtown business leaders, argued against this limited proposal. Exhibiting one form of the "unmerciful spirit" pointed to in moral theology, he feared that, if the city had public toilets, homeless people from around the nation would flock to Atlanta to use them. Sweat also indicated that the homeless were not members of society. The lack of toilets, he said, was not an insult to the human dignity of the homeless because their being on the streets already confirmed they had no such dignity.

The hearing did not resolve the issue. The Open Door led demonstrations and handed out leaflets at City Hall and in the downtown area, asking persons to support the opening of public restrooms. They were joined in these actions by additional homeless persons. These efforts culminated in an all night vigil on the steps of city hall. The next day, the City Council approved the placing of one portable toilet in one park. The Open Door was not satisfied with what they saw as a half-hearted measure. They continued their protest. At one point in their demonstrations, Ed Loring carried a toilet into the lobby of city hall. He sat on the toilet, reading the Scriptures, and refused to move until the city signed a contract to build public restrooms at the city operated Day Labor Center. Although he was arrested for disorderly conduct, the city evidently was moved, as funds were appropriated and construction of the restrooms began at the Labor Center.

More recently, the Community has sought to pressure the city to build housing to replace the SROs destroyed by downtown development. In June of 1990, eight people from the Open Door occupied the abandoned Imperial Hotel in downtown Atlanta. A former SRO, the hotel had been purchased by John Portman, a prominent Atlanta architect and developer. Hoping to tear it down for retail development, he closed the hotel. The development never came, and the Imperial stood vacant for ten years. Occasionally, homeless persons would break in and spend a few nights there. The Open Door Community regarded it as a symbol of the failure of city and business leaders to replace SROs, lost to development, with other housing. Their takeover of the Imperial was initially planned to be symbolic. They expected that they would be arrested quickly. They hoped that the publicity would bring some pressure to bear on the city to begin construction of low income housing and, at the very least, to keep its shelters open through the summer.

Shortly after occupying the building, they unfurled a banner across the front of the hotel, stating: "House the Homeless Here." On the street below, other members of the Community and homeless friends picketed with signs. These questioned the way money could be found to develop Underground Atlanta (a shopping and entertainment complex downtown, partially financed with public monies), a new domed stadium, and extensive Olympic facilities, but none could be found for housing the homeless. In a letter sent to Portman, Atlanta Mayor Maynard Jackson, and Joe Martin of Central Atlanta Progress, those occupying the hotel stated that they had "re-opened the building to show you the way to provide single room occupancy housing."

The letter was prophetic. By mid-afternoon, the hotel began to fill with homeless people seeking shelter. By early evening, some seventy people had taken up residency in the Imperial. Portman faced a dilemma. Either removing the squatters, or letting them stay, he had a public relations fiasco on his hands. With the mayor out of town, he hesitated to sign the necessary police complaint to have the protesters removed. Inside the hotel, homeless persons were cleaning up the rooms and then carrying the debris from their renovations out onto the streets. Since the debris was from the hotel, Portman was held responsible by the city for its removal. Threatened with a city citation, he had a bulldozer and large dumpster brought in to remove the growing hill of trash.

Upon his return to the city, Mayor Jackson entered into negotiations with both Portman and the occupiers of the hotel. The Open Door had turned leadership within the hotel over to the homeless who had joined them. The occupation stretched to two weeks. Finally, an agreement of sorts was arranged. The city promised to build 3,500 units of single room occupancy housing over the next three and half years, with the ground breaking for the first units scheduled for the fall. They also promised to open a shelter which the homeless themselves would govern.

Not everyone was satisfied with the agreement. Many felt coerced, since it had been reached under the threat of arrest. Further, the agreement fell short of providing immediate housing,
and Portman himself, along with other developers, had not
been brought to publicly support the building of new SRO
housing. Thus, several persons refused to leave the hotel even
after the agreement. The takeover ended with their arrests.
Since then, the Open Door has continued, through letter writing campaigns and protests, to remind the city of the promises
made for housing. The city, for its part, continues to drag its
feet. No construction has begun.

The Community's response to the mixed results of their protests is similar to what they say about the necessity and the inadequacy of the mercy they offer. Both their efforts for justice
(the inclusion of the homeless as members in society) and their
efforts of mercy are signs of the kingdom which is both present
and not yet fully come. Consequently, they recognize that there
is a certain eschatological character to their actions on behalf of
justice, actions which also express the corporal works of mercy.
Murphy Davis writes:

> How difficult to hear the word that the Gospel calls us to be fail-
> ures. After all, what are we to expect when we are invited to
> follow a homeless wanderer whose best friends were uneducated
> fisherfolk, prostitutes, and other misfits.
>
> It is hard to learn that salvation comes not because our work
> builds steady progress toward the coming of God's kingdom, but
> because God is full of love and grace for us and the whole
> creation.[24]

IV. The Spirituality of the Open Door Community

In recognizing the already and the not yet of the Kingdom,
the Open Door Community lives what Murphy Davis calls "the
painful tension between faithfulness and failure."[25] This tension
is often the impetus for community engagement in the spiritual
works of mercy. In life and work with homeless persons, there is
much need for comforting the sorrowful, bearing wrongs patiently, forgiving injuries, and counseling the doubtful. These
forms of mutual encouragement, sustained by worship, em-
power the Community to maintain its faith-centered view of the
world, even when events conspire to undercut that faith.

One important form of mutual encouragement within the
Open Door is the assigning of "pastoral friends" to Community
members. When persons join the Open Door, they are given a
pastoral friend to guide them in the Community's life and work.

Whether a person is invited in from the streets or comes to the Community by choice from more comfortable circumstances, he or she is counseled, encouraged, or corrected, if need be, by this pastoral friend. For the homeless, much of this pastoral guidance is in the form of encouragement and advice with regard to solving personal difficulties. They are supported in their efforts to overcome addictions, to gain further education, and to acquire job skills.

The worship within the Open Door that grounds the works of mercy takes a variety of forms. The central act of worship is the Sunday evening celebration of the Eucharist. The Eucharist and the corporal works of mercy have long been connected in Church tradition. St. John Chrysostom wrote:

> Have you a desire to honor the body of Christ? Do not pass him by disdainfully when you see Him naked and exposed to the shame of the streets. Do not glorify Him in the Church with garments of silk if you slight him without pity in the streets where He is perishing in cold and nakedness! For He who spoke the word of power, "This is my Body" (Mt 26:26) also said, "I was hungry, and you did not give me to eat . . as long as you did not do it for one of these least ones, you did not do it for me." (Mt 25:42ff.). Therefore let us learn to grasp the truth with love and to honor Christ as he wills it. Show Him the honor which He has prescribed: give your riches to the poor.[26]

Murphy Davis echoes St. John Chrysostom when she writes of the simple pottery bowl and cup the Community uses in its Eucharistic celebrations:

> The vessels are to hold for us the body and blood of Jesus Christ. . . . we pass them to each other even as our brother Jesus passed them to us. We gather round the table because we know something (perhaps not enough, but at least something) about our own weakness and failings and fragility. We know that if we serve the poor it is not because we are good or loving or smart. It is because — and only because — of the love of Jesus Christ that lives within us.
>
> . . . When the confused and hurt disciples walked down the road from Jerusalem to Emmaus, they had lost their sense of purpose and direction. The stranger who joined them on the road eloquently illuminated the scriptures, but still they were confused. It was only when the stranger was welcomed into their home, gave thanks and broke the bread, that they recognized him. And they jumped out of their seats: "Didn't our hearts burn within us?"
>
> When our hearts burn within us we usually figure it was the soup. But regularly we are reminded: in the ongoing work . . . we look up only to discover that Jesus was with us all along.

The simple earthen vessels remind us of so many truths. They remind us that we ourselves are simple earthen vessels created for the simple purpose of holding the life and love that come to us from God. They remind us of the deep connection between the soup bowls and tea cups of our kitchen tables and the pottery bowl and cup of our Eucharistic table. They remind us that community is a fragile gift from God to be held gently with hearts full of gratitude.[27]

The same theme of meeting the Christ we worship in those we serve marks the prayer of the Community each day. Before leaving to serve the Butler Street Breakfast, or opening the door for showers, or ladling soup for lunch, Community members form a circle and pray. Before serving others, they remind each other that it is Christ whom they serve. Often, persons pray for patience, knowing that some who come for soup will have difficult temperaments. The violence of the streets sometimes erupts in violence within the soup kitchen. Christ's presence in a person who is angry and violent is hard to recognize. Handling the anger in such a way as not to exacerbate it, but also to restrain it so that the peace of the soup kitchen is not destroyed, is a delicate task. It requires a careful, patient admonishing of the violent person. Without continual renewal in prayer of the vision of Christ in the homeless, it would be difficult to continue in this work.

It is in Scripture, read at worship and pondered in their weekly Bible study, that the Community finds this vision repeatedly expressed. Not surprisingly, those texts (Isaiah 58:6-7 and Matthew 25:31ff.) which traditionally grounded the list of the corporal works of mercy have eschatological overtones. And, these texts are central to the Open Door's spirituality and its work with the homeless. They are continually aware in their Community life and their work that there is a struggle to enact their faith vision. A partner in the Community, Elizabeth Dede, writes:

. . . the question "Lord, when did we see you?" is a question central to our faith because seeing, recognizing, and understanding are acts of faith as we live in the post-Ascension world. Jesus has left this earth, and we can see him now only with the eyes of faith.

Often at the Open Door we read Matthew 25 and ask the question, "Lord, when did we see you?" In the answer to that question . . . we find a clear explanation of our calling and work: to be faithful to the risen Christ we must feed the hungry, give a drink to the thirsty, receive strangers in our home, give clothes to the naked, take care of the sick, and visit the prisoner.[28]

The Open Door also manifests a spirituality based in the New Testament in that they see the works of mercy as reciprocal. In acts of mercy, both the giver and the receiver are transformed. Christ acts through the giver in meeting the needs of the homeless, but as Ed Loring explains:

> The reality and presence of God is mediated through the presence and suffering of the poor; so that as we live our lives in solidarity with the poor, we are able to discover who God is; and God's reality, changing reality, confronting reality is mediated to our lives and calls us to new life.

Murphy Davis explicitly links this role reversal to Matthew 25. She also refers to Paul's teaching in Second Corinthians, where he draws out the social implications of equality in Christ: "that at the present time your abundance may supply their want, and that their abundance may, in its turn, make up what you lack, thus establishing an equality" (2 Cor 8:14). This text is also foundational for the works of mercy. Murphy reflects Paul's attitude when she observes:

> What we give is rooted in love because of God's hospitality for us. We are not a social service agency. We are all on the receiving end. We are all outsiders made into community, family, friends through Jesus Christ. The basis for this is seen in Second Corinthians where Paul writes that through Jesus, all enemies are made friends of God. Friendship comes from God. We don't give that friendship, but receive it and share it. Then in Matthew 25 we read that when we feed the hungry, we feed Jesus Christ. The way we treat the dirtiest, hungriest, smelliest, drunkest person, is the way we treat God.

The ground of Paul's convictions in Second Corinthians is Jesus' saving action through the Cross and Resurrection. But, Paul does not see salvation as simply a matter of individual souls being saved. Paul repeatedly draws out the social consequences implied by salvation freely given by the grace of God. Most of the members of the Open Door are Protestant and come from traditions emphasizing justification by faith alone. But, their interpretation of justification resists individualistic understandings of the doctrine. Ed Loring explains that justification carries clear social meanings:

> Since "none are righteous, no not one," no person can say, "I am better." No one can say, "I deserve more because I am more talented, or I have worked harder." No one can say "I am more important because I own more, or I am more educated, or I hold this position in society." Given this radical equality in the eyes of God, we as Christians must avoid erecting barriers, and avoid creating and supporting inequalities of wealth, class, status. We

must, if rich, understand that our wealth comes from others and belongs to all who are in need. We must always work against the structures, the institutions in our society that place one above the other in terms of human dignity and worth. We do not all seek to be the same, rather we work to prevent the using of our differences to justify structures of dominance and oppression which place people in categories, and then conclude that people in certain categories do not count.

The social meaning of justification thus leads to corporal works of mercy. But, as I have argued above, it also raises the issue of membership, and this results in political action to press for the inclusion of the homeless as members in our society.

Ed Loring reflects this critical relation between mercy and membership when he writes that the Open Door resists the split "within the camp of [the] socially concerned" between "those who seek to aid hurting persons and others who fight to change the systems of abuse and injustice."[29] He calls this split "the charity-justice polarity, or the bandaids versus root causes approach." He sees charity as both the basis for the work of justice and its ultimate goal. Charity is the fulfillment of justice, since, when Christ returns, "charity will characterize our lives and the demands of justice will be finished." Until that time, Loring argues, we must continue to seek justice, even as we engage in charity.

Concretely, mercy seeks to remove the distance between persons of wealth and poor persons. It seeks an equality of membership in which all participate in the common life of society. The relationships fostered in acts of charity form the basis for life together in community. Such community, or solidarity with the poor, in turn, grounds the struggle for justice. Ed writes, "The energy for the long haul battle with the powers and principalities of death comes from life among, with and on behalf of the poor."[30] Thus, to separate justice from mercy is to separate the seeking of justice from the actual doing of justice. The relationships formed in acts of mercy motivate one to seek justice, to address the structures creating the suffering to which mercy responds. In this light, the corporal works of mercy point to human needs that must be met in justice. These works of mercy judge all attempts at justice, even as they provide the concrete examples of what justice requires. Short of this perfect justice, Christians must act mercifully in the present.

Theologically, this interconnection of mercy and justice is grounded in faith in a God who is Creator, Judge, and Redeemer. As Creator of all, God gives to human life certain fundamental imperatives which define what is necessary for human

life to be good, to be lived in justice. These include such basics
as food, clothing, shelter, and participation in community life,
including work and rest. To deny these to persons is to deny
their membership in human society as intended by God. Such
denials constitute injustice. As Judge, God calls all to account
for their stewardship of earthly goods. How have they provided
for themselves and others from these common goods which
result from their labor within God's creation? Have their production and distribution served to include or to exclude persons
from sharing in creation and its goods?

As Redeemer, God works to heal the brokenness in human
life, the injustice caused by self-regard in human relationships
and the misuse of God's created gifts. In response to this reconciling work of God, all persons are called to embody in their
lives this loving work of reconciliation. Everyone is invited to
seek justice in charity. Since God is One, this call and its claims
are public. Christians, gifted with the Gospel message, are especially called to witness to God's intention for human life revealed in Jesus Christ. They are called to share this life with
others.

Ed Loring discusses this unity of God as Creator, Judge, and
Redeemer in an article, "All God's Children Gotta Have Shoes."
Ed writes about the feet of Lonnie Moss, a homeless man who
had come to live with the Community, but was, at the time, in
the hospital, dying of cancer. Sitting at the end of the hospital
bed, Ed observed Lonnie's feet, deformed from years of bad
shoes and neglect and time on the streets. Such deformation,
Ed reflected, was certainly not part of God's intention for the
world. With this in mind, he traced the way redemption reas-
serts the intention of God in creation, while, as Judge, God
continues to condemn injustice:

> That "all God's children got shoes" is a vision of hope, a prayer
> for the coming of God's kingdom on earth as it is in heaven!
> Shoes are not only necessary items for survival and health; shoes
> are also symbols of human dignity and social justice. Until each
> of us has warm, dry, and comfortable shoes, the feet of God shall
> ache. Where there are those without good shoes, there is injus-
> tice in the system and deep terrible pain among those who suffer
> shoelessness.[31]

Thus, the Open Door, in engaging in the corporal works of
mercy, sees its work as a witness to what justice demands. The
works of mercy make public and moral claim to the goods intended for all in creation, while, at the same time, giving partial
fulfillment to that claim. In this "between time," when the Kingdom is both present and "not yet," neither justice nor charity is

sufficient by itself; both are integral to sharing in the life of God. The corporal works of mercy, which express charity, both presuppose and surpass justice. They embody a vision of the Kingdom, and, consequently, they point to God's justice as intended for creation.

V. Life in the Open Door Community:
The Spiritual Works of Mercy and Membership

To this point, I have focused primarily on the engagement of the Open Door in the corporal works of mercy and their understanding of those works. Without artificially separating the corporal and spiritual works of mercy, I want to shift the discussion towards the latter, as they are embodied in the life of the Community. How does the structure of the Community itself express, not only the corporal, but also the spiritual works of mercy?

Earlier, I indicated that one key motivating factor for moving beyond the shelter work at Clifton Presbyterian Church and beginning the Open Door was the desire to live in community with the homeless poor. The spiritual works of mercy especially emphasize personal relationships. The founders of the Open Door recognized that, to form personal relationships with the homeless, they would have to build bridges of trust over the differences that make persons strangers to one another.

Even in their shelter work, they saw that relationships of this sort require smallness of scale in order to create a community in which love can be fostered. Within the Open Door, they sought a size and style of ministry that would allow personal relationships to develop. Without this attention to the personal and relational, they saw that the physical works of mercy they undertook could become dehumanizing, both for the homeless and for themselves.

Ed observes that personal relationships, grounded in love, require communities of "human scale," where life can be shared. He finds that faith is a crucial component in creating such communities:

> In the absence of love and in specialization, people become objects — objects of our specialty. Marx's insight about workers being alienated from their work can be applied here. When we become alienated from our work, what we produce is seen only as an object over against us. In the same way, I could see the poor only as objects to be manipulated, and so come to despise the very people I hope to love.
>
> The life of faith is personal, not organizational or institutional. To be personal we must find the size which enables us to

work hard and to rest well, but allows us to love one another, know each other's names, histories, joys and wounds. Love moves us forward very slowly and just little by little as Dorothy Day says.

Bigness leads first to depersonalization, then to alienation, on toward hate, and then to violence and war. Smallness is the shape of hospitality. In spaces with small numbers of folk, the poor become subjects of God's kingdom, not the objects of our latest social theories, or even good works.

The smallness of our work, the friendships and love, are not only foundations, but also the goals of our life and work. We cannot separate means and ends.[32]

This personalist approach reflects a tradition of the corporal and spiritual works of mercy.

The Open Door's personalism stands in contrast to the bureaucracy and professionalism of social welfare programs. Bureaucracy has the benefit of being able to address vast social problems, but, by its very nature, it cannot be concerned with the poor as persons. Bureaucracy treats everyone the same according to its rules which are formulated to efficiently place people into certain categories. In this manner, professionals may quickly process a large number of cases. The professional social worker and other experts within a welfare bureaucracy thus operate from a position of power in relation to those who come for help. The result, according to social critic Michael Ignatieff, is that, in their attempt to respect the rights of each individual by treating everyone the same, they demean as human persons those seeking help. The gestures of human concern, the building of personal relationships, which would express respect for the dignity of the person, are eliminated through administrative routine. Since everyone is treated the same, persons are reduced to objects.[33]

The approach of the Open Door is to address homeless persons on a scale that seeks to prevent this depersonalization. Thus, their own political efforts are directed toward projects in which the homeless will shape their own destiny. The takeover of the Imperial Hotel in order to dramatize the need for SRO housing is an example of such an effort. Within the Open Door's own work of hospitality, each person who comes for soup or a shower is personally greeted. The Community has consciously decided not to put up signs that would direct persons where to go and what to do. Personal directions must be given so that the serving of soup and other ministries do not become routinized. Thus, even with large numbers coming for food or showers, Community members develop relationships with persons from the streets.

But, even with the Open Door's attention to scale, certain barriers which continue to be places of struggle remain within the Community. The most obvious barriers with regard to the homeless have been those created by class and status. As shelter providers at Clifton Church those barriers were firmly in place. By forming a community with homeless persons on a long term basis, the founders of the Open Door hoped to weaken such barriers. Through a sharing in the spiritual works of mercy in community, the Open Door hoped to move toward the inclusion of the homeless as members. This has proved to be a difficult process. The simplest way to trace some of this difficulty is to look at the evolution of structures of authority in the Open Door Community.

When they moved into 910 Ponce de Leon, the founders of the Open Door Community were accompanied by several homeless persons who had regularly stayed at the Clifton night shelter. Since then, homeless persons have continually lived as part of the Open Door Community, sharing in its life and work. However, homeless persons invited into the Community initially were not given positions of authority. The founders assumed leadership positions in the Community and designated themselves "partners" in the Open Door. Persons from the streets and prisons who were invited to live in the Community were called "house guests." Others who came by choice to spend extended periods of time as volunteers were appropriately called "resident volunteers." The distinctions implicit in these terms indicate some of the early difficulty the Community had in structuring its belief in full membership for all based in Christ. The barriers between the homeless and those who chose solidarity with the homeless were not easily erased. The partners and resident volunteers typically have been white, middle class, and well educated. The homeless who enter the Community are impoverished, usually African-American, and often poorly educated.

In the first few years of the Community's existence, these different modes of belonging corresponded to different levels of responsibility and authority within the Open Door. Decision making is, of course, a key facet of membership. Such power is necessary for full participation in the shaping of the life of a community.[34] The difficulty in sharing power was tied to the difficulty of building enduring relationships of trust. Given such different backgrounds, this trust was hard to create. The different levels of belonging represented various levels of responsibil-

ity for the ongoing life of the Community. The founders
believed those deeply committed to the life needed to have more
authority than the less committed. As Murphy Davis put it:

> We reached a point of realizing people bring a variety of agendas
> to the Open Door; and most of them leave after a while. So,
> we're not going to be mean and harsh, but we are going to be
> realistic. The partners are the only ones committed to being here
> next year and beyond. Therefore there are some things we're not
> going to sit up all night debating.

Faced with this realization, the Community developed three
circles of decision making, corresponding to the three types of
belonging. The partners formed the first circle as the "leadership team" of the Community. They made the long-term policy
decisions affecting the ongoing mission, purpose, and stability
of the Open Door. Their decisions came from a process of consensus. Neither resident volunteers nor house guests attended
the meetings of the leadership team.

The second circle of authority included the resident volunteers. Along with the partners, they participated in the "weekly
ministries meeting." Decisions in this circle addressed the daily
operation of the Community, such as work schedules. Here
again, consensus served as the method of decision making.
Partners, however, reserved the power to decide whether an issue belonged in the area of long-term policy or not. If an issue
did belong there, it was tabled until the next leadership team
meeting.

The third circle of authority extended to include house
guests. At a monthly "house meeting," everyone in the Community gathered to discuss and decide issues raised by the house
guests. But again, partners had the power to decide whether
such an issue was appropriate for this meeting or one of the
other circles of authority. Beyond this limitation, the process of
consensus remained the form of decision making.

The relation of the three types of belonging and their corresponding circles of authority remained a sensitive point within
the Open Door. The structure brought a needed order to its life
and work, but it also struck many within the Community as
somewhat contrary to their convictions concerning the dignity
and equality of the homeless. To participate fully in common
life, "house guests" had to have more authority within the Community. Thus, at one house meeting in 1987, a house guest ob-
jected to the structure, saying, "I don't know how you can have a
real community when half of the people here [the house guests]
have no decision-making position."

Murphy Davis answered this challenge to the structure of the Community by emphasizing that the house meeting was a decision making body. Issues could be brought up and decided at house meetings. She continued in her response to stress the religious and moral basis for full participation:

> House policy is formed out of the common discipline embraced by the partners and resident volunteers in response to the call of Jesus Christ. Decision-making authority comes out of that shared commitment. Since house guests do not share this commitment, they cannot fully share in the authority of the house.

Several house guests responded that, as far as they were concerned, they had all the responsibility they wanted at this time. They found a necessary structure to their lives at the Open Door. One stated, "The Open Door is a kind of sanctuary from the powers that beat us down; that put us on the streets and kept us there. I need rest more than I need responsibility right now." The public discussion ended there. The house guest who had first raised the issue did not challenge these statements. Shortly thereafter, she found work and left the Community. But, the issue she had raised continued to be discussed among house guests, resident volunteers, and partners.

Not long after this meeting, I raised the question with Ed Loring whether he thought the Open Door was repeating the patterns of membership and exclusion found in the larger society. He found that the divisions both remained in the Open Door, but were also being challenged by the life of the Community:

> One of the ways I'm impressed with the power of evil is that after so many tries, and so many struggles, class structure still remains. I used to be embarassed about the class distinctions between me and Jay (who was then a house guest). But as I see what is going on in this society, it is radical that Jay and I live in the same house; Jay and I eat at the same table; Jay and I worship the same God. That's about as good as you can discover in North American society today. That doesn't mean I'm giving up and settling for that—I pray, I work, I try to repent of privilege and class-mindedness in my own life. But I'm not thinking now, as I was five, six, or seven years ago, that we're going to pull off a kind of equality and mutuality inside this house that we can't do outside this house. The world is too much here.

Ed's response reflects the sense in which he and the Community were admonished and instructed by the words of the house guest. It also reveals that he and others were coming to recognize the ongoing tension between their convictions and the manner in which the Community was structured. Like the tension between love and justice, this tension was spurring continuing efforts to embody more fully the reality of the Kingdom. One could see here that the Kingdom equality sought in the corporal works of mercy was necessarily calling for the equality of the spiritual works of mercy.

In the fall of 1988, the Open Door began to restructure the manner in which authority would be shared. The aim was to more fully include everyone living in the Community in the decision making process. An initial, symbolic change was the first step in this restructuring. Homeless persons invited into the Community would no longer be called "house guests." Instead, they were now considered Community members from the streets.

More importantly, Community members from the streets who had been with the Open Door for more than two years were invited to assume greater leadership within the house. Relationships with these members from the streets were such that it was foolish to extend greater trust and responsibility to a new resident volunteer than to those from the streets who had been with the Community for a long period of time. This leadership was given structural expression through the creation of a more inclusive type of partnership in the Community. Persons from the streets who had lived at the Open Door for more than two years and intended to remain with the Community were now asked to become partners and participate, on a rotating basis, with the other partners on the leadership team.

The other circles of authority also witnessed some change. The weekly ministries meeting now included all members of the Community. The day to day organization of life within the Open Door was now shared by partners, resident volunteers, and members from the streets. The monthly house meetings ceased to be a decision making body and, instead, became the occasion for a special Community meal and the sharing of music.

These changes were significant within the life of the Community. The new partners have taken on further responsibilities within the Open Door and have become more active participants in its life. They organize and lead the soup kitchen, shower line, or Butler Street breakfast. Some have begun to write for the community newspaper, *Hospitality*. Others have become eloquent public spokespersons on homelessness issues within the city. There is more give and take within the meetings of the Community, as the new structure allows for more voice in decision making by those members from the streets.

This is not to say the barriers are gone or the tensions have disappeared. A Community member from the streets recently told me that he still sees divisions in the house: "A new resident volunteer still has more say than a guy from the streets who has lived in the Community for six months or a year." Still, he appreciated the changes and felt his own sense of membership was stronger:

> At least here when you're different you're still valued. You're still treated like a person. The virtue of this place is that it shows we can live together—black and white, poor and privileged—if we respect each other and give each other a chance.

The recognition of equal personhood in the mercy of God, which is central to both the corporal and spiritual works of mercy, is further seen in the change in perspective that occurred among those who had already been partners.

One partner wrote that she found that a new equality with the new partners was liberating for her. Matthew 25's insistence on the presence of Christ in each person was coming alive for her within the Community itself:

> I had lived and worked with Jay, Carl, Willie, Willie Dee, Ralph and Robert for three years, yet I hadn't recognized fully their partnership with me; I hadn't seen completely how they were my family. Acknowledging their partnership publicly was my first step towards sight, and now I know that I had been blinded by the things that make me different from these new partners: my education, the color of my skin, my comfortable existence, and the privilege to choose to come to the Open Door. But with the eyes of faith, given to us by our brother Jesus, we can see Jesus in everyone, and so recognize our partnership together.[35]

These changes have brought the Community closer to their own convictions of membership, based on the presence of Christ in all and on the sharing of life in Christ expressed in the corporal and spiritual works of mercy. In order for the Community to move toward this sharing, it was necessary that the mutual recognition of need take place. By sharing in a life formed by the practice of the corporal and spiritual works of mercy, they slowly bridged the divisions of class and race expressed in homelessness. In this manner, the Open Door engaged in a continual seeking for community in which all could participate in decision making and thus become full and equal members.

By creating such a community, the Open Door provides a space in which persons from the streets, along with persons from the mainstream of society, can together reclaim a dignity and humanity stripped away by the larger society. In this space, the spiritual works of mercy, expressed in a common life that involves counsel, correction, and patient bearing with each other, help create and sustain healing relationships. As one member of the Open Door from the streets put it:

> Living in community helps support my efforts to live right. It's not easy to do right when you're out on the streets. No one cares and you can't either. Here I'm learning to care again. That's not easy either, but it's the right thing and that makes it seem easier. Knowing other people care. what happens to me helps me care again.

But, the failures in Community and the discouragement the Community experiences, both within and outside, continue. The vision of faith and human failure remain in tension. And, these especially need to be addressed in prayer, in worship, in the Scriptures, and in sacrament.

VI. Conclusion

I have sought, in my description of the relation between the works of mercy and the work of the Open Door Community with the homeless, to emphasize certain themes. First among these is the grounding of both the corporal and spiritual works of mercy in the love (charity) of God for all of us: "We love because God first loved us" (1John 4:19). The works of mercy are the response of Christian faith to God's love. This starting point is crucial, not only for the theological reason of reminding us that we do not save ourselves, but also for undergirding the goal of mercy: equality and mutuality in love. The works of mercy do not seek to establish and maintain the superiority of the merciful over those receiving mercy. Rather, they seek to extend the reconciliation of God offered in Jesus Christ. In a situation of brokenness, the works of mercy intercede to renew God's intent for human relationships.

Second, this grounding of the works of mercy in the love of God means that prayer, Scripture, and common worship are necessary to sustain these works. Without our continual renewal in the love of God experienced in prayer, our efforts at mercy become dry and barren. The result is both "burn out" and the degradation of those toward whom we seek to be merciful. The works of mercy are part of a process of growing in the love of God. Without the nourishment of prayer, the Scriptures, and the Eucharist, we would falter in these works. We may become unmerciful, fearing the homeless, loathing their weaknesses, or asserting with pride that they are to blame for their problems. It is an unmerciful spirit that says I have no responsibility toward human suffering.

The manifestation of such an unmerciful spirit in the depersonalization of the homeless highlights the third theme, the emphasis on the personal. The works of mercy, in seeking to create relationships of mutuality and equality, demand attention to persons in all their uniqueness and diversity. This emphasis on the personal is perhaps most difficult in our society. In terms of homelessness, the very breadth of the issue and its complexity can be paralyzing. Given the intertwining of the structural and personal factors that contribute to homelessness, one is tempted to leave it to the experts and to programs that can be developed on a national scale, or to just simply leave it. There are legitimate worries that shelters and soup kitchens, run by churches or by groups like the Open Door, simply allow society as a whole to evade its responsibility for the homeless. But, these concerns cannot prevent one from acting. To act by offering shelter or soup is to resist; it is to say that you find this situation intolerable. Importantly, it also says to the homeless person that he or she is a human being with dignity, a person whose needs should be met.

The political statement made by this personal action of mercy carries with it the imperative to speak publicly. In an attempt to raise up and clarify this imperative, I have discussed the relationship between love and justice expressed as the relationship between mercy and membership. Love both expresses justice and points beyond it. The acts of mercy seek to build community by addressing human needs, while, at the same time, revealing where our society is unjust. In public actions of protest, these injustices are dramatically presented, with the hope that enough people will respond to effect change. But, without a grounding in specific acts of mercy, these acts of protest would ring hollow. How can one advocate membership for the homeless when one has not begun to embody that membership in acts of mercy?

Appropriately, the final theme I want to raise up here is the eschatological. Christians engaged in the works of mercy live in an in-between time. The justice sought in political action cannot, short of the Kingdom, replace the works of mercy. The Open Door struggles to give institutional expression to its convictions of equality and mutuality with the homeless. Some of the homeless persons who come to the soup kitchen are not very Christ-like in their demeanor. Resistance within society and by public officials to seemingly easy suggestions for addressing some of the needs of the homeless, like public restrooms, remains strong. Millions of dollars will be spent in Atlanta on the Olympics, while homeless persons continue to die of exposure. Nationally, little attention is being given to the adversity people are experiencing as a result of ineffective or nonexistent governmental response to deep economic changes.

In the face of failure, the promise of the Kingdom appears remote. Yet, what sustains hope is found both in the very work which often is so discouraging and in the spirit experienced in the relationships of a Community given over to God's service. Murphy Davis explains that this is possible because the work is sustained by God's love:

> Out of the work the community has formed, and the work has sustained the life of the community. When we feed the hungry and shelter the homeless, we are doing that to Jesus Christ; then we are strengthened in the doing of the task. It's not like the work is a drain and then we need energy for community. Again and again the grace and forgiveness for the community has come to us through the hungry, through the homeless.
>
> In life among the homeless, in taking on the suffering of other people, of having the privilege of sharing the suffering of people who are very deeply hurt and oppressed there is a fruit of joy. It's not something you go after, because that's ridiculous. You don't think of going into places of suffering to look for joy. But it's one of the funny Gospel twists that in following this suffering this other fruit pops up.
>
> There again I think is Matthew 25: when we go to be with the marginalized then the promise is we'll see the face of Jesus Christ. Well, what could that represent except joy? Everything that is associated with Christ is liberation, salvation, healing. Those are qualities that bring joy. We're given the joy to sustain us in the suffering. It's hard to talk about, the joy comes in certain times and in certain ways while we walk through some very painful things.

For the Open Door, the joy of the Kingdom most often comes in the personal relationships fostered as the Community practices the works of mercy. Those who share in these works, either as givers or recipients, find their humanity renewed. These human works depend upon the love of God already present, and they witness to that love in a world marked by sin and hatred. Their seeming weakness and insignificance are transformed by the love of God which makes them part of a greater, final reality. As Ed Loring has put it:

> What the Open Door has been most blessed to do is that it participates in the coming of the Kingdom. And the Kingdom comes and it flees. If you come over here and try to catch it . . . it would elude you. But it's here. I don't want to claim any more

than a mustard seed, but I'm not embarrassed to claim a mustard seed. The Open Door is a mustard seed. And what is so wonderful about mustard seeds is that they are revolutionary.

NOTES

[1]Karl Rahner provides a contemporary theological treatment of this point. See Karl Rahner, "Reflections on the Unity of the Love of Neighbor and the Love of God," in *Theological Investigations, Volume 6* (Baltimore: Helicon Press, 1969), 231-49.

[2]Sidney Callahan, in *With All Our Heart and Mind* (New York: Crossroad, 1988), refers to several Scripture passages in relation to each of the spiritual works of mercy: (1) Admonish the sinner: Mt 18:15; Col 3:16; (2) Instruct the ignorant: Phil 4:8; Rom 14:7; (3) Counsel the doubtful: Jude 1:23; 1 Peter 3:15; (4) Comfort the sorrowful: Is 66:33; John 16:22; (5) Bear wrongs patiently: 1 Peter 2:20-25; (6) Forgive all injuries: Col 3:13-14; (7) Pray for the living and the dead: Eph 6:18; John 5:9; Phil 4:6.

[3]I have been involved with the Open Door Community and its work with the homeless since the spring of 1987. Over the past four years, my involvement has included a six weeks' stay with the Community as a resident volunteer, weekly participation in one of their feeding ministries, and periodically sharing in their retreats, worship, and protests. Additionally, I have conducted intensive interviews with the founders of the Community and a variety of Community members.

[4]For a brief review and critique of recent attempts to count the numbers of homeless, see Richard P. Appelbaum, "Counting the Homeless," in *Homelessness in the United States, Volume II: Data and Issues*, ed. Jamshid A. Momeni (New York: Greenwood Press, 1990), 1-16.

[5]John R. Belcher and Frederick A. DiBlasio, *Helping the Homeless: Where Do We Go from Here?* (Lexington, Massachusetts: Lexington, 1990), 3.

[6]Peter Rossi, *Without Shelter: Homelessness in the 1980's* (New York: Priority Press Publications, 1989), 25.

[7]Michael Walzer, *Spheres of Justice: A Defense of Pluralism and Equality* (New York: Basic Books, 1983). See especially chapters two and three for his discussion of membership. In this essay I have found Walzer's category of membership helpful in analyzing the situation of the homeless in American society. I do not think, however, this analysis necessarily requires agreement with Walzer's entire theory of justice, nor do I use that theory here to talk about homelessness.

[8]A number of studies emphasize that housing issues are at the center of homelessness. See, for example, Elizabeth D. Huttman, "Homelessness as a Long-Term Housing Problem in America," in *Homelessness in the United States, Volume II: Data and Issues*, ed. Jamshid A. Momeni (New York: Greenwood Press, 1990), 81-94; John R. Belcher and Frederick A. DiBlasio, *Helping the Homeless: Where Do We Go from Here?* (Lexington, Massachusetts: Lexington, 1990); Peter Rossi,

Without Shelter: Homelessness in the 1980's (New York: Priority Press, 1989).

⁹Belcher and DiBlasio, 12.

¹⁰Steve Cleghorn, "A State of Emergency," *Hospitality* 5 (March/April, 1986), 10-11.

¹¹R. Bruce Wiegand, "Sweat and Blood: Sources of Income on a Southern Skid Row," in *Homelessness in the United States*, 115.

¹²Walzer, 52.

¹³Cheryl Gorder reports the following statistics regarding the ill health of the homeless: 16.4% had upper respiratory infections; 9.5% had injuries and poisonings; 8.4% had problems with the nervous system; 8.2% had skin disorders; 7.9% had problems with their circulatory system; 6% had problems with their digestive system; and 1.6% to 6.8% of homeless people have clinically active tuberculosis. See *Homelessness: Without Addresses in America* (Tempe, Arizona: Bluebird Publishing, 1988), 117.

¹⁴Ed Loring, "Homelessness is Hell," *Hospitality* 6 (September, 1987), 1-2.

¹⁵Walzer, 32.

¹⁶Ibid., 33.

¹⁷John A. McHugh and Charles J. Callan, *Moral Theology: A Complete Course* (New York: Joseph F. Wagner, Inc., 1958), 490.

¹⁸Ibid.

¹⁹Walzer, 59.

²⁰Plu Tribble, "Druid Hills Church Program Gives Street People a Break," *Atlanta Journal*, 7 February 1980.

²¹Ed Loring, "Washing," *Hospitality* 1 (September, 1982), 3.

²²Murphy Davis, "Easter Comes Even When We're Shut Out in the Storm," *Hospitality* 5 (March/April, 1986), 1-3.

²³The latest demonstration by the Open Door on this issue started at the Imperial Hotel. A march from the hotel to the mayor's office ended with the presentation of a over-sized copy of the city's agreement to begin construction of an SRO by September 1, 1990. Mayor Jackson was not at his office. Ironically, he was at a ground breaking ceremony for the construction of a new McDonald's restaurant. In this moment, the causes of homelessness related to economic change and the lack of appropriate governmental response were symbolically united.

²⁴Murphy Davis, "Nine-Ten," *Hospitality* 4 (November, 1985), 14.

²⁵Murphy Davis, "Easter Comes Even When We're Shut Out in the Storm," *Hospitality* 5 (March/April, 1986), 1.

²⁶John Chrysostom, quoted in Bernard Haring, *The Law of Christ* (Westminster, Maryland: The Newman Press, 1963), 393.

²⁷Murphy Davis, "A Gift of Earthen Vessels," *Hospitality* 4 (August, 1985), 1-2.

²⁸Elizabeth Dede, "When Did We See You?," *Hospitality* 8 (June, 1989), 6.

²⁹Ed Loring, "In Defense of Bandaids," *Hospitality* 7 (November, 1988), 1-3.

³⁰Ibid., 2.

[31]Ed Loring, "All God's Children Gotta Have Shoes," *Hospitality* 2 (March, 1983), 1-2.

[32]Ed Loring, "Let Us Be Small," *Hospitality* 3 (March, 1984), 4-5.

[33]Michael Ignatieff, *The Needs of Strangers* (London: Hogarth Press, 1984), 13-16.

[34]Walzer, 60-61.

[35]Dede, 6.

Ransoming the Captive: Some Perspectives on Ministry in Criminal Justice

Gerald A. McHugh, Jr.

I. INTRODUCTION

The problems of the American penal system and our reliance upon imprisonment of large numbers of offenders as the principal means of dealing with crime are well known. As of 1990, the United States had both the highest rate of incarceration in the Western World and, in absolute numbers, the largest inmate population. The social and economic forces resulting in this situation have been exhaustively documented in a variety of sources and have been the subject of much attention in popular media.

This essay does not seek to address the problems of criminal justice as a matter of political science or sociology, but, rather, to examine the fundamental premises which underlie our thinking about the problems of crime and punishment and their implications for ministry from a theological standpoint.

It is particularly appropriate that these subjects be the focus of theological inquiry, because Christian theology and the Church have been the source of inspiration and support for many of the traditions of penology and the criminal law. Such phenomena as the popular acceptance of criminal law as a moral code, belief in the absolute right of the State to punish offenders, belief in the justness of punishment as a moral matter, and the practice of imprisonment itself, have derived no small measure of force and legitimacy from Christian thought and practice. However, beliefs and practices born with good intentions during an Age of Faith become distorted over time into self sustaining cultural myths and institutions, deriving their legitimacy from worthy goals long since abandoned.

Because of the unique role which the Church and religious thinking have played in contributing to the development of American penal practice, there is a need to distill the historical ingredients behind our thinking on the subject of crime and punishment; to recognize the ways in which theological concepts have been used and abused; and to expose the subtle changes in goals which have evolved over the course of time. It is only by understanding these historical forces and trends that it is possible to think clearly about the subject. The following is a brief review of some of the critical events affecting our thinking on crime.

II. HISTORICAL ANTECEDENTS

A. The Early Church

It is commonly supposed that the biblical command to visit prisoners is the logical point of departure in thinking about the problem of criminal justice. Such an approach would actually be misleading, however, for, as British scholar A.E. Harvey has observed, in biblical times

> prison was not regarded as a necessary element in the penal system and therefore in the administration of justice itself . . . it was essentially no different from the lot of a prisoner of war — and the same words are used in Hebrew and Greek for military, political and judicial prisoners. None of them had the connotation implicit in our word "convict."[1]

The first New Testament reference which seems to address directly the problem of crime as we understand it comes in Paul's letter to the Corinthians, in which he berates them for taking disputes to civil courts: "The very fact that you have legal disputes among yourselves shows that you have failed completely. Would it not be better for you to be wronged? Would it not be better for you to be robbed?" (I Corinthians, 6:1-11). In Paul's view, resignation to wrongdoing reflected the Christian ideal.

This view was undoubtedly reinforced by the social reality that Christians were, to a large extent, isolated from many kinds of worldly affairs. The *Apostolic Constitutions,* one of the earliest formal bodies of law governing the Church, specifically warned against participation in the institutions of civil justice:

"Let not the heathen therefore know of your differences among one another, nor do you receive unbelievers as witnesses against yourself, nor be judged by them, nor owe them anything on account of tribute or fear."[2]

This viewpoint was undoubtedly influenced by the eschatology which prevailed at the time. Because most early believers expected that the Second Coming was imminent, issues of social structure and control were of greatly reduced concern. Partly as a result of this viewpoint, Christian thought about crime began to focus, not upon the act committed and its effects, but, rather, upon the offender individually. As one scholar described the system of law which predated Christianity, criminal codes were largely "objective" in nature.[3] They focused upon the offense committed and prescribed a set penalty for each crime, regardless of intent or circumstances. Murder, as an example, might be penalized by the payment of a fine to the victim's family, with the social purpose of avoiding blood feuds and the religious purpose of appeasing the gods. With Christianity, there arose a "subjective" attitude toward crime: "While previously the law recognized only the injury to the individual or society — that is, the material crime in its direct effect — the ecclesiastical law looked to the soul of the man who had committed the crime."[4] Such thinking, together with the origins of later, philosophically developed Christian thought on free will, served to spiritualize the notion of wrongdoing.

Such thinking worked well within the confines of a religious community. For, so long as Christians remained a minority sect, often persecuted by secular authorities, there was little conflict between religious conceptions of wrongdoing and the way Christians managed temporal affairs.[5] The development of Christianity into a mainstream religion affiliated with political power, however, would necessarily have a dramatic impact upon Christian thought about the problem of crime and the exercise of political power in dealing with it. The watershed event was the reign of Constantine, whose embrace of Christianity as not simply his personal religion, but as a symbol of the Empire, immersed the Church in civil affairs. Many traditional practices of the Empire, such as crucifixion, were abolished as a result of Constantine's conversion, and Roman law became, for the first time, an instrument for the improvement of public morality, with, as one scholar describes it, "its inevitable concomitant, a growing confusion between the notions of crime and sin."[6] Structurally, the most radical change probably consisted of the Emperor's authorization of Church courts to engage in civil litigation, as a result of which the Church became directly involved in administering the law of the Roman Empire.[7] What was started by Constantine was finished by Theodosius, who proclaimed that all Roman citizens must profess Christianity and condemned non-believers with civil, rather than divine, penalties. The office of the Emperor was gradually considered to be sacred itself, so that an offense against the Empire was not just a crime, but sacrilege. The result of this Church-State alliance was hardly the baptism of the Roman Empire. To the contrary, "to envision the faith as a political principle was not so much to Christianize civilization as to 'civilize' Christianity; it was not to consecrate human institutions to the service of God but rather to identify God with the maintenance of human institutions."[8]

The most important result in terms of conceptual thinking was the assumption that any exercise of civil power represented an extension of divine justice and that any offender against the State broke divine law as well. This is not to suggest that Church leaders became simply mouthpieces of the Empire. Ambrose, bishop of Milan,[9] and Augustine frequently intervened in civil matters in an attempt to temper the harsher exercises of the power of the State. In one infamous case involving the murder of some of his friends, to avoid a sentence of death, Augustine wrote directly to the judge to plead for the offenders' lives:

> . . . by no means permit this to be done. For although we might silently pass over the execution of criminals brought up for trial not by an accusation of ours . . . we do not wish the sufferings of the servants of God avenged by the infliction of precisely similar injuries in the way of retaliation. Fulfill, Christian judge, the duty of an affectionate father; let your indignation against their crimes be tempered by considerations of humanity; be not provoked by the atrocity of their sinful deeds to gratify the passion of revenge, but rather be moved by the wounds which these deeds have inflicted on their own souls to exercise a desire to heal them.[10]

There is also evidence that many citizens recognized Church courts as being more fair and less brutal than those directly administered by the Empire.[11] On balance, however, the development of Christianity into a religion affiliated with the centers of power marked the beginning of a radical shift in viewpoint in the way in which people would come to think about the problems of crime and punishment.

B.   The Middle Ages

The collapse of the Roman Empire involved the Church in the maintenance of social order far more directly than anyone observing the beginnings of Christianity would have supposed. As English historian Richard Southern has suggested, "the Middle Ages may be defined as the period in Western European history when the Church could reasonably claim to be the one true state, and when men . . . acted on the assumption that the Church had an overriding political authority."[12] In part, this had to do with the Church's filling the vacuum left in the absence of any political authority, and, in part, it had to do with the internal development of the Church and the growth of such institutions as Canon Law. The birth of Canon Law provided the Church with a highly detailed, precise code for governing virtually all aspects of Christian life, but it did not simply regulate Church affairs. Rather, the Church, regarding itself as the greatest of all of the civilizing institutions of the world, undertook many of the social and economic tasks which, in modern times, have come within the competence of the State.[13]

Medieval theologians began to consider directly the origin of political power, and the State came to be viewed as an integral part of the natural order of existence. Aquinas, for example, saw the exercise of political power as necessary to permit human beings to fulfill their political and social nature, and came to view the social regulation created by law as consistent with the divine law of revelation and the natural law of creation, expounded in his writings.[14] Bonaventure, for another, probably reacting to the chaos of the Middle Ages, saw the authority of the State as necessary to prevent sinful humankind from chaos and destruction.[15]

During the Inquisition, the alliance between the Church and temporal authority grew, as the Church was dependent upon government to carry out the sentences imposed by the Inquisitors. Technically, the Church was prohibited by Canon Law from shedding blood. When capital punishment was decreed, it was necessary for the State to carry out the execution, and a prince would be automatically excommunicated for failure to execute a heretic. In order to transfer the responsibility for the death to the State, Church officials would plead for mercy, which the prince, mindful of his spiritual duty, would refuse.[16]

The identification of temporal and divine power was not diminished by the Reformation. Martin Luther, in trying to reconcile the teaching of the New Testament with the political reality of his day, resorted to a dual system of public and private morality, under which governmental enforcement of criminal law, by whatever means, was one form of adhering to God's will, just as acts of personal morality were another.[17] John Calvin, the other great reformer, taught that the State and the law

should be made use of by Christianity, both to promote maintenance of the true religion and to promote the public good.[18]

The change in thinking which occurred over time can aptly
be illustrated by the writings of Aquinas on the subject of heresy, a sin he described as meriting "not only excommunication
but also death, for it is worse to corrupt the faith which is the life
of the soul than to issue counterfeit coins which minister to the
secular life. Since counterfeiters are justly killed by princes as
enemies to the common good, so heretics deserve the same punishment."[19]

What is most remarkable about passages like this is not simply the change in spirit which they reflect, as contrasted to the
tolerance of Paul and Augustine, but the way in which the legitimacy of political power is assumed and becomes the basis for
justification of a Church practice. An ironic transformation occurred. Christianity had become deeply involved in temporal
affairs, and, as a result of that process, the exercise of civil authority assumed divine status. As the influence of the Church
declined, however, and power flowed back to civil authorities,
there was no change in the view that the exercise of civil power
reflected God's will. As legal scholar Nicholas Kittrie has written:

> Crime and sin continue to be inextricably merged . . . from the
> foggy interface of the state and church in this period evolved the
> concept that certain acts were punishable as crimes if they of-
> fended the temporal regimes represented by the prince . . . the
> facility with which the sovereign's army could be turned into po-
> lice insured that thereafter offenders and punishments would be
> handled by the state. This transfer of functions, however, re-
> flected little change in the public attitude that "God's will" was
> served by present and earthly punishment, a belief that provided
> both executioner and spectator with the feeling that they were
> directly involved in "the Lord's work."[20]

The quote from Aquinas also reflects significant change in
theological thinking. Among early Christians, the function of
law was clearly the direction of believers to a closer relationship
with God and among themselves. In Medieval thinking, the focus shifted away from the human to the abstract. Crime, as an
idea, no longer represented the injury which one human being
inflicted on another; rather, it primarily signified the violation
of a metaphysical order, and the right of civil authority to enforce the law by whatever means necessary became entrenched.
The criminal law shifted back to an objective code, in which

offenders and their relationship to the community were no longer a primary focus.

C. The American Tradition

Modern American penal practice also has religious roots, found in the contrasting views toward crime and punishment held by Puritan and Quaker colonists. The Puritans, who viewed themselves as a "sacred remnant" people, intended to establish a State based upon their religious beliefs. Law was used to advance those beliefs, to punish those who denigrated them, and to enforce what the Puritans believed to be proper standards of moral behavior. The identification of crime with sin in Puritan society was complete, and criminal penalties were attached to a variety of offenses against religion, such as speaking against the Bible.

A Calvinist emphasis on the sinfulness of human beings and the need for authority to keep them from temptation made the criminal law an institution of particular importance in Puritan society: "Authority of the state was thus religiously condoned. Carried to its conclusion, this meant that the welfare of the whole, rather than the individual was the chief concern of the state."[21] Punishment of crime had several purposes in Puritan society, but reformation of offenders was not one of them. Rather, punishment of crime was justified as protection of the community and vindication of God's law on earth. Nowhere was this more evident than in the practice of an execution sermon, in which a minister would preach on an appropriate subject while a condemned prisoner waited upon the gallows.[22]

The Quaker conception of law, on the other hand, was radically different. To begin with, the Quakers were not so concerned with social conformity, having been the victims of persecution under English law, and carefully incorporated a tolerant spirit into their system of governance. As a reform measure, in substitution for the English system of corporal and capital punishment, the Quakers instituted a system of prisons and workhouses for convicted criminals.

The Quaker penal model was an explicitly religious one, with emphasis on the reformation of criminals. The Quakers believed that criminal punishment should not be vindictive in character, but rather should be imposed in a way which would persuade an offender to change.[23] The concept of the penitentiary was literally a place where one would be confined in order to find repentance, modeled in part after monastic prisons from the Middle Ages. In the Quaker view, crime represented as much a failing of society as it did of the individual, and part of

the purpose of imprisonment was to isolate offenders from con-
taminating influences. Here is the way David Rothman, a sociologist, describes the penitentiary:

> Convinced that deviancy was primarily the result of the corrup-
> tions pervading the community, and that organizations like the
> family and the Church were not counterbalancing them, they
> believed that a setting which removed the offender from all
> temptations and substituted a steady and regular regimen would
> reform him. Since the convict was not inherently depraved, but
> the victim of an upbringing that had failed to provide protection
> against the vices that loosen society, a well-ordered institution
> could successfully reeducate and rehabilitate him.[24]

The reformist vision which led to the use of imprisonment as
the primary method of punishment in American society quickly
evaporated. Merely isolating offenders from the community
proved to have little effect, and prison officials began to experi-
ment with more punitive measures. Solitary confinement and
hard labor, enforced by corporal punishment, were then employed in a variety of institutions as means of influencing behavior. This harsher régime has been described as "an insurgent
and reactionary movement against the failure of the first prison
system . . . a system replete with severity, regularity, perpetual
silence and the domination by prison authorities of the inmates'
body and spirit."[25] Over time, confidence in the underlying assumptions of the penitentiary system dissolved, and it survived
only as a physical plant for the confinement of inmates. By that
time, however, the notion that imprisonment was the most effective means of punishment of crime was deeply entrenched in
the American legal system, and imprisonment continued as the
primary method of punishing crime in America, with little
thought given to the original premises upon which it started.

Toward the end of the nineteenth century, dissatisfaction with
the American prison system led to a reform movement spear-
headed by a coalition of prison officials, criminologists, ministers, and others. The first Congress of the National Prison
Association, now known as the American Correctional Association, took place in 1870, and evidenced a peculiar intermingling
of the religious fervor of earlier reformers and the scientific approach of modern criminologists. This reform movement assumed that prisons, when properly administered, could succeed
in the reeducation of criminal offenders to turn them from a life
of crime. However high the ideals of the reform movement, in
practice lasting prison reform has never taken hold in the
United States. As one commentator described it,

the sustaining belief in the reformability of the inmate waned. All that was left . . . was the order of solitude and labor. In the penitentiary system, the inmate was rendered unsocial. That was supposed to be a means to the end of reformation. When the end collapsed, the means survived, and prisons continued to try to cut the inmate off from his social roots.[26]

Modern penal practice is characterized by a lack of direction, as described by former Attorney General Ramsey Clark:

We cannot say that we practice any theory of penology in America today. We do what we do. And what we do has practically no relationship to what we say we do. Essentially we use penology — without saying so — to confine and thus separate for a time people who have committed crime. Simultaneously we punish by providing an unpleasant experience.[27]

Notwithstanding this lack of direction, however, and lack of success, new prisons continue to be built and inmate populations continue to expand.

III. MODERN IDEOLOGIES UNDERLYING CRIMINAL JUSTICE

Living in a secular age, we find that there are no overtly religious models for criminal justice, such as those which inspired penal practices among the Quakers and other early reformers. Rather, contemporary justifications for imprisonment rest upon two competing philosophies: retribution and deterrence. This section will address some of the key premises underlying both theories in order to identify the difficulty in accepting either as an appropriate view.

In general, the fundamental premise of retribution is that those who commit evil acts or crimes *deserve* to suffer punishment as a matter of right or justice. In popular terms, this might be reflected in the sentiment, "he had it coming to him," but this frontier sense of justice actually has far deeper intellectual roots.

One popular understanding of retribution is similar to the original Puritan notion that punishment for crime represents righteous vengeance against wrongdoing. The Biblical concept of *lex talionis,* or the law of retaliation, is interpreted literally as being a component of divine justice. Evangelist Billy Graham's famous remark that rapists ought to be castrated is a perfect example of this blend of populist sentiment legitimized with a religious gloss. In fact, the tendency to cite the *lex talionis* is one of the classic examples of misapplication of a theological concept in defense of penal practice. Scriptural scholars have long since concluded that the Old Testament prescription of "an eye for an eye, a tooth for a tooth" was hardly a divine imperative. Rather, it was a limit upon human vengeance, which was intended to limit retaliation for wrongdoing and thereby avoid an escalating spiral of violence.[28] In fact, the *lex talionis* represented an advance in law, in that its true purpose was to insure a sense of proportionality between an offense and its remedy.

Even within the Old Testament itself, strict retaliation was not prescribed. As one historian has observed:

> In the oldest text, that of Exodus, [the *lex talionis*] is in fact followed immediately by a law which orders the liberation of a slave in compensation for the loss of an eye or a tooth (Ex. 21:26-27), and it is preceded by a law which, for an injury inflicted in a fight, orders only the payment of a compensation and medical expenses (Ex. 21:18-19). Only in one case is strict retaliation exacted: the guilty murderer must die and cannot buy his freedom. This rigor is justified by a religious reason: the blood which has been shed has profaned the land in which Yahweh dwells (Nb. 35:31-34).[29]

It is particularly noteworthy that the Israelite code prohibited the taking of life, except for an offense against God, because the nation of Israel was a theocracy, much like the Roman Church during the Middle Ages, in which the law of the State was coextensive with the law of the religious community. Consequently, it is hardly valid to draw conclusions pertinent to modern, secular institutions from Old Testament Israel.

Retribution theory takes far more sophisticated and principled forms than the notion of divinely-sanctioned vengeance. One famous defense of retribution came from Pope Pius XII, in a 1954 address to the Italian Association of Jurists. Pius contended that the civil punishment of criminals was justified because it was consistent with metaphysical concepts of justice:

> . . . the order violated by the criminal act demands the restoration and reestablishment of the equilibrium which has been disturbed. It is the proper task of law to guard and preserve the harmony between duty on the one hand, and law, on the other, and to reestablish this harmony if it has been injured . . . This order of duty is necessarily an expression of the order of being, of the order of the true and the good, which alone has the right of existence, in opposition to error and evil, which represent that which should not exist.[30]

Consistent with the Canon Law tradition, Pius further argued that punishment of criminals could also have a reformative effect in the same way that spiritual penances would.

This defense of the concept of retribution repeats the same error of Medieval theologians, crediting the civil authorities with purposes consistent with divine law. In a theocracy, the shared beliefs of the community lent some credence to this view. In a modern society, characterized by pluralism and a fundamental feeling of alienation on the part of large numbers of people, the likelihood that there is spiritual value derived by an offender is questionable. This is particularly true where, as a simple matter of statistics, the poor, powerless, and minorities are far more likely to be arrested, prosecuted, and actually imprisoned, than are mainstream members of society accused of crime. Sociologist Jackson Toby of Rutgers University has observed that punishment serves the goals of rehabilitation, or, in Canonical terms, is "medicinal," only "for those offenders who regard punishment as a deserved deprivation resulting from their own misbehavior . . . A child who is spanked by his father and the member of a gang who is jailed for carrying concealed weapons are both 'punished', but one accepts the deprivation as legitimate, and the other bows before superior force."[31]

In the final analysis, concepts of retribution are unacceptable in thinking about the problem of crime from a theological standpoint for two reasons. First, as Pius' defense illustrates, retribution theory is rooted in principles which fail to take into account the reality of the modern world and rely upon an abstract, philosophical concept of justice which is inconsistent with the Biblical ideal. In Biblical terms, justice represented the proper relationship between God and His people in the context of a community of believers who shared common ideals. An integral part of the prophetic notion of justice conveyed in Scripture is that of social reform and equality. Old Testament prophets were "impetuous writers such as we of the present day should denounce as anarchists and socialists. They were fanatic in the cause of social justice, and loudly proclaimed that if the world were not just, or capable of becoming so, it had better be destroyed. . ."[32]

Focusing on the philosophical concept of retribution diminishes the idea of justice. Distributive justice, or social justice, concerned with the general allocation of resources and benefits in society, is overlooked, while retributive justice, focused on individual acts of wrongdoing, becomes the predominant concern. This artificial distinction, which is alien to Biblical thought, divorces the problem of crime from broader issues of social inequities and from the problem in community life which crime fundamentally represents. Attention to "paying back" wrongdoers and restoring an abstract order of justice, while necessary to achieve the civil goal of maintaining social order, is incompatible with fundamental Christian values.

The second fatal flaw of retribution lies in its reliance upon the concept of desert, which is explicitly repudiated in the New Testament. The *lex talionis* was explicitly rejected by Jesus (Matt. 5:38-39), and condemnation of others is specifically forbidden (Luke 6:37). Certain parables in the New Testament go so far as to endorse what conventional wisdom would deem to be an injustice. For instance, in Matthew 20:1-16, the master of the vineyard pays workers the same wage regardless of whether they work equally, or, as Matthew's Gospel further recognized, God "makes his sun to shine on good and bad people alike, and gives rain to those who do good and those who do evil" (Matt. 5:45). The right to exact vengeance, to punish, is reserved to God. In view of these theological precedents, the view of retribution theorists that civil justice mirrors divine justice makes sense only if one persists in a medieval world view.

The second contemporary justification for punishment is deterrence. In popular culture, it is widely accepted that the principal purpose of punishment of crime is to make an example of convicted offenders for the purpose of inhibiting criminal conduct on the part of others. Deterrence theory is so deeply entrenched in our approach to criminal justice that it is little known that deterrence as a justification for punishment has its roots in the Utilitarian philosophy of Jeremy Bentham and other nineteenth century theorists whose focus was the proper relationship of individuals to society. Bentham and others recognized the imposition of punishment on any individual as an intrinsic wrong in the sense that, by definition, a punishment amounts to infliction of pain on a human being. Bentham reasoned, however, that such a wrong could be morally justified where it served a greater good; namely, the prevention of further acts of wrongdoing by others. The fundamental premise in all Utilitarian philosophy was that the needs of individuals necessarily must be sacrificed for the common good:

> The principal end of punishment is to prevent like offenses . . . The offense already committed concerns only a single individual; similar offenses may affect all. In many cases it is impossible to redress the evil that is done; but is always possible to take away the will to repeat it; however great may be the advantage of the offense, the evil of the punishment may always be made to outweigh it.[33]

The logic of deterrence suggests that, if a punishment of one level of severity is not sufficient, then a greater level of severity is justified. One prominent proponent of deterrence theory has defended the use of capital punishment by arguing that "though we have no proof of the positive deterrence of the [death] penalty, we also have no proof of zero, or negative effectiveness . . . Our moral obligation is to risk the possible ineffectiveness of execution."[34]

From the standpoint of social utility, choices are frequently made that vindicate the rights of one group or one individual at the expense of another. A former Director General of the Swedish National Prison Board has clearly identified the risk presented by Utilitarian philosophers:

> From the crisis standpoint of social utility, many people are "worthless" — in fact this word is much too vague, the truth being that many individuals are physically, mentally, or morally a burden to society and sometimes a permanent and heavy one. There exists no rational reason to provide for them, or to provide expensive care . . . Much money could be saved if one could get rid of them or at least reduce the costs of maintenance to the minimum.[35]

From a theological standpoint, in contrast, no individual can ever be treated as a means to an end. To the contrary, if the Christian tradition stands for any principle, it is the affirmation of the worth of each individual. It follows that a Utilitarian social ethic is obviously incompatible with the person centered ministry of Jesus described in the New Testament. The parables of the Lost Sheep (Luke 15:1-7), the Lost Coin (Luke 15:8-10), and the Prodigal Son (Luke 15:11-32), emphasize the value of the individual as against the group, notwithstanding the depths of any given individual's sinfulness. Certainly, part of the scandal of Jesus' association with tax collectors, publicans, and adulterers was the possibility that his acceptance could be construed as condoning their activities. If Christian faith is to stand opposed to any tenet of prevailing culture, then it must, at a minimum, affirm the worth of individuals, in spite of the judgments of society.

Popular acceptance of the values of deterrence is consistent with the Utilitarian values of our society as a whole. As Jacques Maritain has pointed out in his criticism of Western democracies, the most widely accepted understanding of the common good is simply "bourgeois materialism, according to which the entire duty of society consists in seeing that the freedom of each one is respected, thereby enabling the strong freely to oppress the weak."[36] In Christian terms, Maritain argues, a concept of common good must necessarily require mutual interdependence between individuals and the community at large, in which the needs of each individual member must be respected.

Not surprisingly, Maritain sees this skewed concept of what constitutes the common good as related to a failure to address issues of distributive justice.[37]

To summarize, the prevailing concepts used in thinking about the problem of crime, and society's response to it, leave much to be desired from the standpoint of Christian values.

IV. LIMITING PREMISES FOR MINISTRY IN CRIMINAL JUSTICE

The history of Church involvement in the development of Western and American penal practice should give us reason to pause in suggesting, with any great confidence, an approach to ministry. Experience suggests that the wiser course is to proceed from limiting assumptions about the role which ministry can play in addressing such problems. First, there is the undeniable reality of crime as a problem. The once popular liberal sentiment that all criminals are wholly victims themselves has been discredited by events. The need to protect victims of crime, many of whom are the most helpless members of our society — the elderly, children, poor, and minorities, does not permit us the luxury of sentimentalism in thinking about the problem. In recognizing the need to combat crime, however, we make the same historical mistake as generations ago if we are equally naive in assuming that the criminal law acts as an agent of justice in any Christian sense of the word. Criminal law is essentially a means of social control which, in the reality of every day application, is often divorced from any meaningful concept of justice. Attempting to baptize secular institutions will simply lead us down the same troubled path which began with the reign of Constantine.

A secular *system* of law is incapable of reflecting religious values. The institutions of criminal justice should be viewed as a necessary evil, existing by virtue of the fact that evil is a reality in the world. When we attempt to ascribe some higher purpose to them, we lose sight of how limited they are in their ability to meet human needs and also lose sight of how imperfectly these institutions are capable of addressing broader issues of justice. This does not mean that the Church should treat as irrelevant the practices of courts and prisons or that it should not seek to exert influence over such institutions in order to make them as humane as it possibly can. It simply means that we should not harbor any illusions about the true purposes of such institutions and should not extend to them greater legitimacy than that to which they are entitled.

A similar sense of realism should cause us to recognize the reasons for popular anger about, and fear of, crime and its consequences. Retaliation in the face of wrongdoing is a natural human instinct. If this were not the case, Jesus' ministry would have been in vain. An approach to criminal justice ministry which fails to take into account the immense sufferings of the victims of crime and the evil inflicted by criminal wrongdoing is both unrealistic and unfairly narrow in scope.

In the final analysis, the continued existence of crime and our inability to deal with it in a meaningful way is a profound sign of the disorder which marks our existence. Virtually any broad pronouncement which purports to recognize justice in the context of our contemporary legal system is presumptuous in the extreme. Our penal system does not serve the public, the needs of offenders, or the human needs of those who administer it, whether they be the judges who impose sentences or the correctional officers who carry them out. The depth of our failure counsels, above all, a sense of humility about our inability to address the situation, and, at all costs, we should avoid the conceit that our institutions reflect any divine order. Rather, we should approach a ministry in the field of criminal justice with the recognition that we are dealing with flawed institutions, performing a necessary function to the satisfaction of no one. As Reinhold Niebuhr has warned, analysis of any social problem must be based upon "Christian humility which has no illusions about our ideals and structures or about the realities of the community."[38]

V. FOUNDATIONS FOR A CHRISTIAN MINISTRY IN CRIMINAL JUSTICE

A. Love of Enemies

The cornerstone of criminal justice ministry lies in the concept of love of enemies. In the first instance, this teaching is appropriate because of its realism. In a tragically real way, many criminals and people in prison (although, by no means, all) are enemies to society and enemies to us individually in the sense that anyone is a potential victim of crime. The preceding sections of this essay have emphasized the degree to which social injustice is at the root of much crime. It defies belief, however, to suggest that every criminal is a harmless, misunderstood victim of oppression. While many criminals are victims to some degree, many are also victimizers who prey upon others. Criminals, like all human beings, can be destructive, hostile, dangerous individuals. If we refuse to recognize the harsher realities involved in crime, we are not confronting life as it exists.

Unwillingness to recognize the harsher realities of crime also undermines the truly radical character of Christian faith. Jesus was, among many other things, a realist. He did not teach, "do not have enemies," as well he might. Rather, the invitation of the Gospel is far more difficult: In full awareness of the fact that one has enemies, or potential enemies, love them anyway. The Gospel does not deny the existence of evil; rather, it mandates that, in spite of it, we should return evil with good. Sentimentalism about crime sidesteps one of the most difficult challenges of faith.

Individuals who, in the name of charity, prefer to remain naive about the harsher realities of crime also deny criminals their dignity as human beings. Those who would treat criminals solely as victims have, in effect, concluded that criminals are wholly subject to deterministic forces which deprive them of the ability to choose. While this may be so in the case of the criminally insane, the vast majority of criminal offenders do not easily fit within any classical definition of mental illness. Similarly, while much crime is related to substance abuse and particular acts are driven by the forces of addiction, the ability to make a fundamental choice about another way of life still exists, as witnessed by the many people who succeed in conquering addictions. To deny that criminals have the same ability to choose as others is to refuse to accord them an equal status as human beings.

Aside from its realism, the concept of enmity is appropriate in analyzing the problem of a response to crime in that it is a relational concept, indicating whether individuals or groups of people are reconciled or at odds. The designation "enemy" is not a definitive label; it merely describes the stance between individuals at a given point in time. For, an ally today may be an enemy tomorrow, and the opposite is also true.

We have relatively little difficulty accepting this concept in the context of international relations or politics. In fact, a cynic would suggest that, in modern society, the speed and frequency of shifting alliances are such that the concept has no meaning whatsoever. As a society, however, we are far less willing to recognize the possibility of a change in relationship between criminals and society. The stigma of a criminal conviction is something which lasts a lifetime. An offender goes from being a convict to being an ex-convict, and such a designation is an inherent limit on all of the other options in life. An ex-convict cannot vote, cannot enter many professions, is precluded from military service and entrance to many educational institutions, and, as a practical matter, without lying about his or her past, is actively discriminated against in the job market.

Using the concept of enmity to analyze crime involves opposition to the prevailing wisdom that criminals should be permanently isolated and denied any participation in community life. To approach crime in this way is to conceive of it as a problem of human interrelationship and to recognize the possibility that the break in that relationship, which crime represents, can be addressed.

The notion that criminals should be treated as enemies is easily admitted by most people. The notion that the Gospel commands us to "love" them regardless is hardly likely to be as easily accepted. In considering any social problem, one realizes that the suggestion that Christian love has any relevance would, at first, seem to be foolish idealism. Unless we are willing to concede, however, that the Gospel has no relevance to the "real world," then necessarily we must consider what the command to love means in the context of the problem of crime. Theologian Bernard Haring contends that the ethic of love, as expressed in the Sermon on the Mount, is a "normative" value for Christians, requiring them to evaluate every aspect of their lives in terms of that commandment.[39] The same sense of realism which causes us to recognize the harsh realities of crime might lead us to conclude that it is nonsensical to speak of love in terms of addressing the problem. But, approaching the problem from such a perspective would mean certain concrete things.

First, it means a recognition of criminals as human beings who possess dignity and, whatever their conduct, deserve a measure of respect simply by virtue of their being fellow humans. An insight from Gabriel Marcel underlines this point. Marcel believes that, before people can bring themselves to participate in destructive actions against others, it is first necessary for them to deny the humanity of the people who will suffer as a result:

> I [must] lose all awareness of the individual reality of the being whom I may be led to destroy. In order to transform him into a mere impersonal target, it is absolutely necessary to convert him into an abstraction: *the* communist, *the* anti-fascist, *the* fascist and so on . . .[40]

Typically, we engage in similar thinking about crime. The fear of becoming a victim of crime and the stereotypes about criminal behavior perpetrated by the media allow us to have an image of wrongdoers as dangerous deviants, a view which we

144

believe applies universally. In fact, any one with close contact with our criminal justice system recognizes that the backgrounds, personalities, values, and abilities of the criminal population are, in many ways, mirror images of our society at large. For example, murder is, ironically, still most likely to be committed by someone well known to the victim, and murderers, as a rule, are the least likely to have a prior criminal record or to commit the offense again.[41] While it is difficult to conceive of criminals as individuals and fellow human beings, such knowledge is essential to our willingness to address crime in other than a punitive way.

It follows that Christian teaching requires us to refuse to return evil with evil and to reject the logic of the worse the crime, the harsher the punishment. Even in practical terms, the emphasis on vengeance has not proved successful. Mandatory sentencing and longer terms have meant only more and larger prisons, not less crime. As noted in several instances above, this does not mean that it is unnecessary to protect the community from crime, only that the form of protection chosen should take into account the need to reintegrate the offender into the community. In this regard, "good theology" makes good sense, because virtually every offender is at some point released. Unless we are willing to fund and maintain a virtually limitless system of prisons, almost all of those sentenced to confinement will be released some day. If we can finally bring ourselves to accept the fact that ever harsher punishment has not proved effective in stemming the tide of crime, then we will have taken the first step toward restructuring our means of dealing with it.

Beyond principled opposition to purely vindictive responses to crime, which will be discussed in more detail in the next section, concern for reconciling offenders with the community requires concrete means of reaching out — as volunteer teachers inside prisons, intermediaries between convicts and families outside, prospective employers for offenders upon release, et cetera. What is important is not so much the specific method employed, but, rather, the effort to bring offenders back into the community, which, of course, serves the interest of society as well as of the individual.

The difficulty in accomplishing such reintegration leads to another important characteristic of Christian love: it is unconditional. Jesus did not teach a love of others because of the benefits it will bring. To the contrary, he warns us that such an approach to life is as likely to bring suffering as it is to bring reward. To embrace New Testament values on this subject is something one does in spite of the consequences.

It is the unconditional nature of Jesus' teaching that makes it most difficult to comprehend. In part, the reason is that, in popular terms, the concept of "love" is most often viewed as strictly an emotion, or what philosophers would term romantic or erotic love. In theological terms, in contrast, love constitutes a spiritual outlook, a fundamental attitude toward life, stemming, not from emotion, but, rather, from the decision to make a commitment to what is, in the final analysis, an article of faith. In that sense, the problems of criminal justice are a uniquely appropriate subject for theological study. It is impossible to "love" criminals in any conventional sense of the word. Common experience and our natural instincts lead us in directly opposite directions. It is only by a conscious act of will that we are able to look beyond these instincts in order to adhere to a more fundamental truth.

If it is true that love of God and others is the overriding Christian value, then it is also obvious that it is a mistake ever to consider any particular social or political institution as genuinely "Christian." As Emil Brunner has observed: "Love is always related to persons, never to things. We can speak of a just law or system, but we cannot speak of a loving law or system."[42] The ends of secular justice — maintaining social order, protecting victims, giving expression to prevailing values — may, at any particular point in history, be more or less consistent with Christian values. In the final analysis, however, from a Christian standpoint, there remains an overriding importance of each individual, a fact which must be respected, notwithstanding the needs of the group.

Recognition of such limits runs the risk of assuming that there is a dual standard of ethics or morality: one for public and one for private affairs. It would be more accurate to say that there is in many areas a convergence of public and religious values, but the inherent limitations on all human institutions will always prevent the religious ideal from being achieved or expressed in the context of any social system. The best illustration I can provide for this concept is that of a federal judge, now deceased, who enforced the law in as humane a way as it was possible, without shrinking from his obligations, but would simultaneously maintain contact with dozens of men whom he had sentenced in an attempt to assist them in returning to the community.

B. Forgiveness and Reconciliation
A parallel of the ethic of love is that of forgiveness. Jesus taught: "Do not judge others, and God will not judge you; do

not condemn others, and God will not condemn you; forgive others, and God will forgive you" (Luke 6:37). Obviously, if any element of New Testament teaching is relevant for a Christian perspective on criminal justice, then it is forgiveness, although, again, the notion of forgiveness is alien to popular thought. Given the harsh effects of crime, the concept of forgiveness seems, at first glance, every bit as unreal as the concept of love of enemies. As noted above, however, unless we are willing to concede the irrelevance of the Gospel for confronting social problems, it is necessary to come to grips with forgiveness in the context of criminal justice.

It is a cherished myth of American culture that criminals "pay their debt to society" and then go free. This is false on two counts. First, as suggested above, a criminal conviction can be stigmatizing for life. Second, and perhaps more importantly, the same problems of distributive justice which cause crime to occur, if not more frequently, then more openly, among the poor and disadvantaged, remain problems once a criminal has served his or her sentence. Aside from depriving offenders of their liberty for a period of time following imposition of sentence, we do little, either in prisons or upon release, to change the patterns leading to crime in the first place.

In religious terms, these problems amount to a lack of forgiveness, because forgiveness necessarily implies a willingness to restore with an offender the relationship which has been damaged by his or her offense. Failure to recognize the need for forgiveness and the reconciliation which comes with it results in an escalating spiral of criminal conduct simultaneously fueled by both criminals and society. Crimes occur which threaten society, resulting in criminal punishment which has as its principal purpose the isolation of criminals from the community and its members. But, this isolation is temporary, and an offender is returned to the community without addressing any of the fundamental problems contributing to crime in the first place, whether such problems originate with the offender or with the community. The likelihood is that an offender will commit further crimes, and society now indignantly responds with still harsher punishments, increasing the isolation of the offender from the community and creating a self perpetuating cycle which makes any genuine reconciliation less probable over time. Jesus' warning that those who do not forgive will not be forgiven takes on an ironic meaning when viewed in this context, because career criminals are no more willing to forgive what they perceive to be society's wrongs against them than we, as a society, are willing to forgive their conduct.

Perhaps most important of all, an ethic of forgiveness is directed to the future. The causes of crime are complex and varied, and what serves as an explanation in one case will not serve in another. The despair and poverty which lead an illiterate and unskilled man to drug addiction do not suffice to explain similar conduct coming from a child born to affluence, and, yet, drug addiction and the criminal conduct which stems from it cut across all class boundaries. The economic needs which impel a welfare mother to shoplift do not motivate the exact same conduct on the part of an economically independent professional. Sexual assault is equally reprehensible, whether committed in a random attack by a habitual offender or in the confines of a private college fraternity. In each instance, once the social goal of preventing such conduct has been met, the far more important issue is the way to reconcile that offender with the community, as this is also the best method of minimizing the chances that the offense will happen again. Assigning blame is a necessary function of criminal law. It is not, however, consistent with a Christian world view, and, ironically, beyond the point of protecting the victims of crime, it is counterproductive socially because of its preoccupation with the past rather than with the future.

One could well object that, in virtually every instance in the New Testament, sinners came to Jesus, actively seeking forgiveness, whereas many criminals feel no need of forgiveness for themselves. Superficially, this is often true, for many prisoners are anything but apologetic for their actions. Rather, they often exhibit a threatening or arrogant posture. In practical terms, this attitude is frequently a defensive veneer which seeks to obscure profound feelings of worthlessness:

> It is sometimes claimed that many criminals are so alienated from conforming society and so identified with a criminal subculture that moral condemnation, disapproval, or rejection by legitimate society do not touch them; they are, it is said, indifferent . . . at least as far as the moral stigma of being criminal is concerned. Possibly this is true for a small number of offenders. . . . For the great majority of prisoners, however, the evidence suggests that neither alienation from the ranks of society nor involvement in a system of criminal values is sufficient to eliminate the threat to the prisoner's ego posed by society's rejection. . . . The wall which seals off the criminal, the contaminated man, is a constant threat to the prisoner's self-conception and the threat is daily repeated in reminders that he must be kept apart from 'decent men.'[43]

This type of hostility is but a manifestation of the continuing spiral described above, in which offenders cope in part by "rejecting the rejectors."[44] Or, as criminologist David Matza has described this phenomenon, a convict "excuses himself, but his gruff manner has obscured the fundamental sense in which he begs our pardon."[45]

It is also doubtless true that, in a significant number of instances, criminals neither seek nor want reconciliation with the community. It seems clear, however, that Jesus' call to extend forgiveness was not naive, but radical. He himself was, in starkest terms, the victim of murder at the hands of the Roman Empire, but forgave his executioners, while teaching his followers to forgive, not seven times, but "seventy times seven" (Matt. 18:22). This highlights yet another area in which Christian thought departs from secular thinking. Civil justice permits the chronic or most serious offender to be abandoned, whether it be by the ultimate penalty of execution or by a life sentence without possibility of parole. In social terms, such sanctions represent a final break with an offender, denying any possibility of reconciliation with the community at large. The New Testament would seem to forbid Christians the luxury of such final solutions, no matter how reprehensible the crime or how persistent the offender. Once again, therefore, the logical absurdity of believing in a "Christian" system of law becomes clear. Law demands accountability and, therefore, sanctions, making a "forgiving" legal system an impossibility by the nature of law itself.

VI. THE SHAPE OF CHRISTIAN MINISTRY

The conclusion which emerges from the tangled role which Christianity has had in influencing criminal law and penal practice, as contrasted to the dictates of the Gospel, is that Christians do not bear witness to what they believe through the institutions of criminal justice. In fact, it is impossible to do so, for the nature of such institutions is necessarily inconsistent with the values which the Gospel calls upon Christians to profess. To bear witness in the context of criminal justice must be the function of ministry, understood in the broadest sense, encompassing not only traditional forms of ministry, but any manner of reaching out to address the problems of crime.

Historically, in the early Church, ministry in the context of "criminal justice" was shaped within a community of shared values, in which the role of ministry was to return an offender to the common path which the community sought to follow.

Thereafter, within the context of a Church operating within society at large, ministry came to be understood as the business of effecting conversions among criminal offenders, with the optimistic goal of directing them from a life of crime to a life of faith. More recently, ministry has come to be understood by many as a form of rehabilitation, in support of the social goals of the prison system itself. Each of these different forms of ministry is limited by its particular social context.

The remarkable spirit of the early Church, while a source of inspiration, is not easily recaptured in a world in which Christianity is a mainstream institution with its own 2,000 year history for which to answer. The notion that the primary goal of ministry is to secure formal conversions to religious faith is unworkable in a pluralistic society where tolerance of diversity and competing beliefs is a necessity. The more modern assumption that ministry is simply an adjunct to social service demeans faith as simply another form of therapy.

In Biblical terms, we are told that Jesus represented freedom to prisoners. The Letter to the Hebrews proclaims that Jesus has, in fact, already brought freedom to prisoners (Heb. 10:34; 13:3). This represents fulfillment of the promise of Isaiah, that the Messiah would "proclaim liberty to the captives and release to the prisoners" (Isaiah 61:1).

Obviously, this freedom cannot be understood to mean freedom in a physical sense, because Jesus freed no captives, except metaphorically. Reduced to simplest terms, the New Testament promise of freedom is a promise of freedom from condemnation for wrongdoing and, simultaneously, a promise of the possibility of reconciliation. Christian ministry in criminal justice is but a tangible sign of the possibility of such reconciliation.

Traditional models of ministry and, more recently, fundamentalist models, have been content simply to preach the possibility of reconciliation as a spiritual matter to prisoners. While such a model of ministry has undeniable appeal to many people, it suffers on two counts. First, in a secular world, religious language and symbolism have questionable meaning to large numbers of the population. Cynicism about the function of organized religion is such that preaching alone, in the absence of tangible actions which convey the meaning behind the words, is likely to have little effect. Second, traditional preaching models of ministry almost invariably fall into the trap of retributivism, focusing upon the acts of individual offenders, in isolation for the community at large. Such a model of ministry fails to take into account the need for tangible efforts at reconciliation between offenders and the community, which, apart from their social utility, are a concrete sign of the possibility of deeper spiritual reconciliation. A model of ministry which fails to incorporate such activism runs the risk, not only of being ineffective, but irrelevant in terms of bearing witness to what should be most fundamental in a Christian response to crime.

The concrete form which such ministry takes is far less important than the values it is meant to express. Victim-offender reconciliation programs, designed to communicate clearly to criminals the consequences of their actions, while inviting victims to extend some measure of forgiveness, have successfully been pursued both in this country and in Canada.[46] Programs to educate offenders away from violence,[47] and to deal with the particular problems presented by sexual offenders,[48] exist. Models for restoring family relationships between incarcerated offenders and their spouses and children have been established.[49] Individual congregations have sponsored residential training programs for ex-offenders to provide them with needed support to reintegrate themselves into the community. The national leadership of some denominations has committed them to finding alternative methods for addressing the problem of crime.[50] What is lacking is not paths to follow, but people to travel them.

Ministry in criminal justice is not concerned simply with offenders and their victims, and the reconciliation which occurs between them. It is also concerned with those outside the walls who are ostensibly the beneficiaries of the criminal justice system. The Letter to the Hebrews, concerning prison ministry, is most frequently translated as "remember those who are in prison, as though you were in prison with them" (Heb. 13:3). Scripture scholar, A. E. Harvey, has pointed out that a more literal translation of the original Greek text expresses a more profound insight: "Remember those in prison, for you are prisoners with them yourselves."[51] If the latter translation is the correct one, it is reminding us that the way in which we respond to the reality of evil, and treat criminals, is as much a statement about ourselves as it is about those whom we condemn. To the extent that we subscribe to the prevailing belief that ever harsher retribution is the most appropriate means of dealing with crime, we are, in effect, condemning ourselves to the seemingly endless spiral of crime and punishment which has proved fruitless to date. While it is illusory to suggest that there is any answer to the problem of crime, and it is not the primary function of ministry to solve social problems as such, the failure to recognize what faith demands of us is, in its own way, a judgment upon ourselves.

NOTES

[1]A.E. Harvey, "Custody and the Ministry to Prisoners," *Theology* 78 (1975): 82.

[2]"Apostolic Constitutions," *The Ante-Nicene Fathers*, ed. Rev. Alexander Roberts and James Donaldson, Vol. VII (Buffalo, New York: The Christian Literature Co., 1886), Chapter XIV, 381.

[3]Raymond Salielles, *The Individualization of Punishment* (Boston: Little, Brown, and Co., 1913), 30-34.

[4]Ibid., 37.

[5]See, generally, Massey H. Shepherd, "Before and After Constantine," in *The Impact of the Church Upon Its Culture*, ed. Jerald Brauer (Chicago: University of Chicago Press, 1968).

[6]Charles Cochrane, *Christianity and Classical Culture* (New York: Oxford University Press, 1944), 203.

[7]Shepherd, *op. cit.*, 26.

[8]Cochrane, *op. cit.*, 336.

[9]Ambrose, *Duties of the Clergy - Book II*, in *Nicene and Post-Nicene Fathers*, ed. Phillip Schaff and Henry Wace, Vol. X (Buffalo, New York: The Christian Literature Co., 1896), Chap. XXI, 59, no. 102.

[10]Ibid., *The Confessions and Letters of St. Augustine*, Vol. I, Letter CXXIII, to Marcellinus (412 A.D.), 470-71.

[11]See Cochrane, *op. cit.*, 204.

[12]R.W. Southern, *Western Society and the Church in the Middle Ages* (Maryland: Penguin Books, 1970), 16.

[13]Edwin R.A. Seligman, ed., *Encyclopedia of the Social Sciences* (New York: MacMillan Co., 1930), s.v. "Canon Law," by H.D. Hazeltine.

[14]Paul E. Sigmund, *Natural Law in Political Thought* (Cambridge, MA: Winthrop Publishers, 1971), Chap. 3 discusses medieval conceptions of natural law.

[15]Bonaventure, *Commentary on Ecclesiastes*, generally. Also Bede Jarnette, O.P., *Social Theories of the Middle Ages 1200-1500* (Maryland: The Newman Book Shop, 1942), especially the chapter on law.

[16]A.S. Turberville, *Medieval Heretics and the Inquisition* (London: Archon Books, 1964), Chap. V, 206-28, discusses penalties for heresy.

[17]Ernst Troeltsch, *The Social Teaching of the Christian Churches*, trans. Olive Wyon (New York: MacMillan Co., 1931), 549.

[18]Ibid., 615. See George Lee Haskins, *Law and Authority in Early Massachusetts* (New York: The MacMillan Co., 1960), for an interesting case study of the application of Calvin's ideas to American colonization.

[19]Thomas Aquinas, *Summa Theologica* (many translations), 2,2, gv. xi, art. 3.

[20]Nicholas Kittrie, *The Right to Be Different, Deviance and Enforced Therapy* (Baltimore, Maryland: Penguin Books, 1973), 13-14.

[21]Richard Quinney, *The Social Reality of Crime* (Boston: Little, Brown and Co., 1970), 64.

[22]David J. Rothman, *The Discovery of the Asylum, Social Order and Disorder in the New Republic* (Boston: Little, Brown and Co., 1971), Chapter 1, generally.

[23]Auguste Jorns, *The Quakers as Pioneers in Social Work*, trans. Thomas Brown (New York: The MacMillan Co., 1931).

[24]Rothman, *op. cit.*, 82.

[25]Orlando Lewis, *The Development of American Prison Customs, 1776-1845* (Montclair, New Jersey: Patterson-Smith, 1967), 78.

[26]Robert M. Senkewicz, "Early American Innocence and the 'Modern' Prison," *America*, April 24, 1976, 355.

[27]Ramsey Clark, *Crime in America* (New York: Simon & Schuster, 1970), 219.

[28]John Sheehan, S.J., *The Threshing Floor, An Interpretation of the Old Testament* (New York: Paulist Press, 1972), 191.

[29]Roland de Vaux, *Ancient Israel* (New York: McGraw-Hill Book Co., Inc., 1961), 149.

[30]Pope Pius XII, "Crime and Punishment," in *Contemporary Punishment: Views, Explanations and Justifications*, ed. Rudolph Gerber and Patrick McAnany (Notre Dame, Indiana: University of Notre Dame Press, 1972), 59-72.

[31]Jackson Toby, "Is Punishment Necessary?," in *Contemporary Punishment: Views, Explanations and Justifications*, 225.

[32]A. Renan, *History of the People of Israel (1894)*, cited in Boaz Cohen, *Law and Tradition in Judaism* (New York: KTAV Publishing House, Inc., 1969), 191-92.

[33]Jeremy Benthan, *Theory of Legislation* (London: Truebner and Co., Ltd., 1904), 272.

[34]Ernest Van den Haag, "On Deterrence and the Death Penalty," *Journal of Criminal Law, Criminology, and Police Science* (1969), 147.

[35]Hardy Goransson, "Human Dignity in the Execution of Punishment," in *Studies in Penology*, ed. Manuel Lopez Key and Charles Germain (The Hague: Martinus Mishoff, 1964), 108.

[36]Jacques Maritain, *The Rights of Man and Natural Law*, trans. Doris C. Anson (New York: Charles Scribner's Sons, 1943), 8.

[37]Ibid., 9.

[38]Reinhold Niebuhr, *Faith and Politics* (New York: George Braziller, 1968), 131.

[39]Bernard Haring, *A Theology of Protest* (New York: Farrar, Straus and Giroux, 1970), 11.

[40]Gabriel Marcel, *Man Against Mass Society* (Chicago: Henry Regnery Co., 1952), 157.

[41]Virginia Mackey, *Restorative Justice — Toward Non-Violence* (Louisville: Presbyterian Church, 1990), 44.

[42]Emil Brunner, *Justice and the Social Order* (New York: Harper & Row, 1945), 16.

[43]Graham Sykes, *The Society of Captives* (Princeton, New Jersey: Princeton University Press, 1958), 66-67.

[44]Lloyd McCorkle and Richard Korn, *Annals of the American Academy of Political and Social Science* 293 (1954): 88.

[45]David Matza, *Delinquency and Drift* (New York: John Wiley and Sons, Inc., 1964), 41.

[46]U.S. Association for Victim-Offender Mediation, 254 South Morgan Blvd., Valparaiso, IN 46383.

[47]Alternatives to Violence Project, Inc., 15 Rutherford Place, New York, NY 10003.

[48]Center for Prevention of Sexual and Domestic Violence, 1914 N. 34th St., Suite 105, Seattle, WA 98103.

[49]Parents Anonymous of Virginia, 1212 Wilmer Avenue, Richmond, VA 23227.

[50]E.g., Prison Violence and Nonviolent Alternatives, 200th General Assembly, Presbyterian Church (U.S.A.) (1988).

[51]A. E. Harvey, *op. cit.*, 87.

Visiting the Sick in the World of Modern Health Care

Doris Gottemoeller, R.S.M.

> Seek for health from Christ, the true light:
> have recourse to the church, be anointed with
> blessed oil.
> **Sermons** of St. Caesarius of Arles (+543)

> Pilgrim-houses, leper-houses, and alm-houses
> or hostelries . . . have been founded and en-
> dowed by the generosity of the faithful.
> **C. 17 of the Council of Vienne,** 1327

> The Sisters admitted to this Religious Congre-
> gation . . . must have in view what is peculi-
> arly characteristic of this Institute . . . that is a
> most serious application to the visitation of the
> sick.
> **Rule of the Sisters of Mercy,** 1831

> The concern that Christ showed for the bodily
> and spiritual welfare of those who are ill is con-
> tinued by the Church in its ministry to the
> sick. This ministry is the common responsibil-
> ity of all Christians, who should visit the sick,
> remember them in prayer, and celebrate the
> sacraments with them.
> **Pastoral Care of the Sick: Rites of Anointing
> and Viaticum,** 1983.

These texts, drawn from different sources in different ages,
hint at how broad and diverse is the Church's interpretation of

155

the words of Jesus: "I was sick and in prison and you visited me" (Mt 26:36). As a Sister of Mercy whose congregation takes visiting the sick as one of its primary objectives, I welcome this opportunity to explore its history and meaning from a contemporary perspective.

That the sick have a special claim on the Christian conscience seems self evident. And yet, today the Church's explicit and public commitment to care for the sick is blurred in focus and diminished in scope. "Visiting the sick" has become the occasional spontaneous act of an individual toward a family member or neighbor, the career choice of some Christians in the healing professions, or a corporate business presided over by a religious congregation. Missing is a sense, in most sectors of the Church, that caring for the sick is integral to living and proclaiming the Gospel and that everyone within the Church shares responsibility for it. As the national Commission on the Catholic Health Care Ministry pointed out in 1988, the Catholic health ministry in the United States is in a state of crisis. Unless bold steps are taken, the Commission said, an essential element of the Church's mission will be diminished and a long history of care for the suffering and needy will be virtually ended.[1]

As we look at the many ways in which the Church has tended to the needs of the sick through the ages, two questions keep recurring, at least implicitly:

What is the meaning of sickness and of health?
What is the purpose of our "visit"?

"Visit," in the second question, refers to any purposeful act, whether spontaneous or organized, to alleviate the distress of those perceived to be sick. As simple as these questions seem, through the centuries opinions have differed widely about the answers, and they will be a recurring theme throughout this essay.

It is my thesis that the contemporary estrangement from this work of mercy is a consequence of uncertainty about the meaning of sickness and of health and about what we as Christians can or should do about it. In order to situate visiting the sick in today's age of high tech, high cost medicine, I plan to (1) examine the Christian tradition of ministry to the sick; (2) identify the contemporary factors which militate against this Gospel imperative; and (3) describe what I see as the Christian responsibility today.

Part One: "Visiting the Sick" in Christian Tradition

1. In the Ministry of Jesus

The story of Jesus's ministry to the sick is almost exclusively a story of miraculous healings. Scripture scholars have analyzed the relevant texts from every angle. This critical literary and linguistic study indicates some probable exaggeration and duplication of events in the miracle stories. It also points to the existence of contemporaneous rabbinic and Hellenistic miracle stories which diminish the uniqueness of some of the events reported in Jesus's life. Form criticism reveals the existence of Hellenistic redactions of earlier Palestinian stories. But, even after strict critical standards have been applied to the texts, there remains a distinct and substantive historical core of healing miracles.[2]

So central to Jesus's work is healing that he describes his entire ministry in these terms: "Go and tell John (the Baptist) what you hear and see: the blind regain their sight, the lame walk, lepers are cleansed, the deaf hear, the dead are raised, and the poor have the good news proclaimed to them" (Mt 11:4-5). Numerous passages describe Jesus's daily activity as a ministry to the sick. For example, Matthew tells us that Jesus began his Galilean ministry by

> . . . teaching in their synagogues, proclaiming the gospel of the kingdom, and curing every disease and illness among the people. His fame spread to all of Syria, and they brought to him all who were sick with various diseases and racked with pain, those who were possessed, lunatics, and paralytics, and he cured them (Mt 4:23-24).

In addition to these summaries, there are the stories of individuals whose cures were occasions of some special teaching. The widow of Nain whose only son had died (Lk 7:11-15), the woman suffering with a hemorrhage who touched his garment (Mt 9:20-22), the man with a withered hand whom Jesus cured on the Sabbath (Mt 12:13), the Syrophoenician woman whose daughter was possessed by a devil and who begged for the metaphorical scrap from the table of the master (Mk 7:25-30), and the paralytic lowered through the roof (Lk 5:18-25) are some incidents that come to mind.

The prominence of healing in Jesus's ministry is both an expression of his compassion and a revelation of God's creative energy manifesting itself through him. Jesus's heart was stirred to pity (Lk 7:13; Mt 9:36) by the sight of suffering. His rhetorical response to the Pharisees in Matthew's house, "Those who are well do not need a physician, but the sick do" (Mk 2:17), justifies his attention to tax collectors and sinners, but also points to the special claim which all suffering people had on his heart.

Jesus's healing was directed to the whole person, not just to the individual's physical health or spiritual well being. When confronted with the man blind since birth (Jn 9:2), he refused to admit that his misfortune was the result of sin. Rather, in his glance Jesus took in the man's total condition and cured both physical and spiritual infirmities. In another example, after forgiving the paralytic's sins, he said, "That you may know the Son of Man has authority to forgive sins on earth, I say to you arise, pick up your mat and go home" (Mt 2:5-12).

Jesus's ministry to the sick was never routinized or impersonal, but always a deeply personal exchange, characterized in the Gospels as a response to faith. So significant was this predisposition that Jesus is described as unable to perform miracles in its absence (Mk 6:5). Indeed, the healing stories may aptly be called faith stories.[3] In these narratives, "Faith meant . . . not confidence in a miracle worker, but confidence in God's disclosure of himself through Jesus."[4] Thus, healing signified the action of God in Jesus, the coming of God's reign (Mt 12:28), or its fulfillment in action (Mt 11:3f.). The revelation of God through Jesus's healing words and deeds was a necessary element of his messianic work.[5]

Moreover, this messianic work was entrusted by Jesus to his followers. Matthew records the commissioning of the Twelve in the words of Jesus, "As you go, make this proclamation, 'the kingdom of heaven is at hand.' Cure the sick, raise the dead, cleanse lepers, drive out demons" (Mt 10:7-8). The continuation of this ministry to the sick in the post resurrection community is amply attested to in the Acts of the Apostles (e.g., 5:15-16; 8:7).

Curing the sick is not only an experience of God's powerful action revealing itself in Jesus and his followers, but it is also a recognition of the unity of all Christians in Christ. In the theology of Paul, the doctrine of the unity of all persons in Christ furnished the Christian community with a powerful motivation for care of the sick. As Paul expresses it, "God has so constructed the body . . . so that there may be no division. . . but that the parts may have the same concern for one another. If (one) part suffers, all the parts suffer with it" (1 Cor: 12:24-26). The enumeration of gifts within the Body of Christ includes the specific gift of healing, which is intended to be informed by love and directed to the betterment of the whole Body.

In the life of Jesus and the early Christian community, then, sickness is any suffering of body or spirit, without regard — and, indeed, without much understanding, given the state of knowledge at the time — for the causes of illness. The response to illness was to restore the sufferer to health, that the power of God acting in and through Jesus and his followers might be revealed and that the reign of God might become visible on earth.

2. In the Life of the Church

Care for the physical and spiritual needs of the sick has continued in a variety of ways from the time of the early community to the present. The responsibilities of the diaconate in the first five centuries included providing refuges for needy persons, such as travelers, the sick, the elderly, widows, orphans, and foundlings.[6] Attestation in Canon Law to the Church's concern for the sick is provided as early as the fourth century in the pseudoapostolic *Canones Arabici Nicaeni* which provided that in every city separate facilities were to be provided for pilgrims, the sick, and the poor.

The history of what were to become known as hospitals dates from the fourth century when St. Basil erected a large institution near Caesarea in Cappadocia. There are records of hospitals in most major cities of Europe and the Christian East from that time on. These institutions were under the supervision of bishops, and their organization varied with the needs of the times. Some were situated in monasteries as an extension of the monastic obligation to hospitality. Indeed, manuscripts dealing with medical matters, still extant in Benedictine monasteries, demonstrate that the monks provided more than just shelter. Other hospitals were located near city cathedrals, where canons regular looked after them, and in rural parishes.

The eleventh and twelfth centuries were an age of momentous increase in the number of hospitals. According to one source, there were nine hundred eighty hospitals in medieval England, their number reaching its maximum in the thirteenth century and diminishing after 1350.[7] The pattern was similar in all Catholic countries, and, by the fourteenth century, such great cities as Rome and Florence had thirty hospitals each.

The eleventh and twelfth centuries also saw the development of organized confraternities of laity, usually living under a religious rule, who dedicated themselves to the care of the sick. Even after towns and communes took some responsibility for the provision of hospitals, they respected the role and structure of these hospital guilds or confraternities: "It was inconceivable in the Middle Ages for any individual or collective work of charity to be excluded from the discipline of ecclesiastical authority."[8] These institutions profited from the generosity of private individuals who not only made financial contributions (frequently in the form of real estate), but also offered their services as nurses, oblates, and lay brothers. Another significant group in the development of medieval hospitals was made up of the military religious orders, such as the Knights Hospitaller of St. John (later the Knights of Malta and the Knights of Rhodes) and the Teutonic Knights. These military orders went to the Holy Land during the Crusades to provide both military assistance and medical care for the sick and wounded. Similar groups were the Hospitallers of St. Lazarus, dedicated specifically to the care of lepers, and the Order of the Holy Spirit, which was specifically dedicated to hospital work.

The rise of the modern State in the fifteenth century saw the consolidation of hospitals into larger, centralized institutions, a movement which required a combination of papal approval, local episcopal authorization, and, in the area of civil jurisdiction, the authorization of the lords. Interestingly, the physical structure of the new centralized hospitals was usually similar to the Hospital of the Holy Spirit, built in Rome in the fifteenth century; they were cruciform, with an altar at the intersection of the four arms for the celebration of the liturgy.

The Reformation brought changes in health service related to the changing religious orientation developing in the various countries.[9] This transformation included the secularization of institutions, the dispersal of religious hospital institutes, and the intervention of absolute kings who opposed the rights of ecclesiastical authorities. Italy was the last of the European countries to effect the transformation. Charitable institutions remained in the hands of the Church there until 1890, when they were transferred to the civil government.

In the New World, the first hospital was established by the conquistadors at Santo Domingo in 1503. The oldest continually existing hospital in this hemisphere is the Hospital de Jésus in Mexico City, founded in 1524. In Canada, the Hôtel-Dieu de Précieux Sang was founded in Quebec in 1639.

In the United States, the Church's ministry to the sick is associated in a large measure with the efforts of women religious. From the early nineteenth century on, sisters committed themselves to the health care of a rapidly growing American population, consisting chiefly of immigrant families.[10] Their efforts included visitation of the sick poor in their homes, the organization of hospitals and homes for the aged, and the instruction of nurses and other health care professionals. Long after hospitals became the accepted venue for treatment of serious illness, sisters continued home visitation, as witnessed by such congregations as the Dominican Sisters of the Sick Poor and the Bon Secours Sisters, founded for this purpose. Until the post-Vatican II changes, every convent of Sisters of Mercy maintained a visitation book in which were noted the visits the sisters made to the sick and bereaved in the parish, after the day's teaching.

Sisters brought health care to mining towns, lumber camps, gold fields, and Indian missions. They treated epidemics of tuberculosis, typhoid, yellow fever, cholera, influenza, smallpox, and diphtheria. They cared for the victims of natural disasters and economic depressions; they treated the wounded of the Civil War and the Spanish American War. Many of them died young, and, almost miraculously, their numbers were replaced.

In the past fifty years, Catholic health ministry in the United States has become increasingly associated with hospitals owned and administered by religious congregations of women or, in a few cases, by congregations of men or by dioceses.[11] We will look further at the consequences of this institutional focus below. Before leaving this historical overview, however, we need to examine two other dimensions of the Church's ministry to the sick: the sacramental and the pastoral.

The ancient ritual of anointing the sick with blessed oil is a good place to begin. There is documentary evidence of the custom of bishops and priests blessing oil to be used for the sick as early as the third century, and ritual texts for the anointing exist from the eighth century.[12] In the early centuries, the anointing was done by the ordinary faithful who took the oil home and applied it to the sick person with their own prayers. The application of oil was generous—to the afflicted part of the body or even to the whole body, if the illness were not localized—and repeated frequently and even daily until health was restored. Several sources show that it was even taken as a drink, especially if the recipient suffered from problems of speech. Beginning in the eighth century, a distinction between the anointing by laity and by clergy gradually came into force, due to the gradual association of anointing with priestly forgiveness of sins and to the elaboration of the various monastic rituals. The emphasis shifted from healing the body to preparing it for death. Anointing came to be known as "Extreme Unction" and to be reserved for situations of imminent death. Sacramental Penance, Extreme Unction, and Eucharist or "Viaticum" were the "Last Sacraments."

Despite this long tradition, Anointing the Sick was not defined as a Sacrament until the Council of Trent.[13] In four canons dealing with the Sacrament, the Council affirmed that (1) Extreme Unction is a Sacrament instituted by Christ and announced by James;[14] (2) it has an enduring salvific meaning in terms of conferring grace, remitting sins, and comforting the sick; (3) the rite and practice of the Sacrament correspond with the scriptural precedent in James; and (4) the proper minister of anointing is an ordained priest. The canons say nothing specific about the rite's function as a Sacrament of the dying or about the degree of illness required. The Council asserted that Anointing is to be administered to the sick, especially to those who are so dangerously ill that they seem near to death. Further, it said that the Sacrament may at times restore bodily health; thus, its benefits include a range of spiritual, psychological, and physical goods.

Twentieth century popes appealed repeatedly for Anointing before the sufferer reached the point of death, but the usual precondition for the administration of the Sacrament continued to be the imminence of death. The morbidity and fatalism attached to the rite meant that most postponed it until they were no longer able to participate consciously in its celebration.

Vatican II restored the earlier notion of the Sacrament as a ministry to the sick and called for a revision of the rite. The resulting *Pastoral Care of the Sick: Rites of Anointing and Viaticum* distinguishes clearly between pastoral care of the sick and of the dying.[15] The former is comprised of visits to the sick, visits to a sick child, communion of the sick, and Anointing of the Sick. The latter includes celebration of Viaticum, commendation of the dying, prayers for the dead, and rites for exceptional circumstances. Furthermore, the various rites are adapted to ordinary celebration within a community of believers, whether during Mass or outside it, to celebration in a hospital or institution, and to emergency situations when time is at a premium. In present practice, the ministries of visiting the sick and bringing Communion to them are done more and more by laity.

Ministry to the sick throughout the ages has focused on caring for physical disease and infirmity, on consoling and counselling those with spiritual ills, especially in the Sacrament of Penance, and on sacramental Anointing of the Sick and the dying. More recently, there has been a growing recognition of the interrelationship among physical, mental, psychological, and spiritual well-being. The emergence of pastoral ministry to the sick as a distinct discipline is one consequence of this awareness.

A recent history of pastoral care names four traditional pastoral functions: healing, sustaining, guiding, and reconciling.[16] They give rise to helping acts by Christian persons toward those whose troubles arise in the context of ultimate meanings and concerns. Pastoral care of the sick attempts to assist troubled persons at a time when illness or infirmity has made them especially open to spiritual insight. The goal is not only physical restoration, but also an integration on a higher spiritual level than it was prior to their illness. Such pastoral ministry has become professionalized today, and pastoral ministers in health care settings typically have had the benefit of specialized preparation in theology, psychological and spiritual counselling, and liturgical arts.

A historical overview of the Church's ministry to the sick must also include mention of the use of prayers to the saints, folklore, charismatic healings, and exorcisms.[17] Prayers to specific saints, application of their relics to diseased organs or bodies, and pilgrimages to their shrines have long been part of Christian tradition. The manner in which a saint died frequently determined the kind of illness he or she was supposed to be able to help. For example, Agatha, an early Christian martyr, was said to have had her breast cut off as she was being executed; therefore, diseases of the female breast traditionally come under her charge. The custom of blessing throats on the feast of St. Blaise is based on an apocryphal tale about his saving a child from choking on a fishbone. The crutches and canes left at the shrines of Lourdes, Fatima, Medegorje, and Guadalupe bear eloquent testimony to those who have found physical healing there; many others have found spiritual solace.

Early and medieval Christian practices also included many remedies based on a mixture of folklore, superstition, and piety. Prayers, ritualistic acts, and consecrated potions were combined to produce what seem like bizarre therapies today. For example, one "medical" book from around the year 1000 prescribes writing scriptural words on the communion paten, mixing therein herbs and consecrated wine and water brought by a virgin, washing off the paten with the liquid, then carrying it to church and praying masses and psalms over it, and finally drinking the potion in the name of the Trinity! (This was to ward off enchantment by elves.)

History also records many stories of charismatic men and women with special healing powers. Saints Martin of Tours, Francis of Assisi, and Elisabeth of Hungary were all noted for their healing miracles. Even in our present age, the healing powers of some holy persons — not excluding doctors — seem to exceed scientific explanation. The surprising growth of the charismatic movement within Catholicism since Vatican II is based in part on the popularity of charismatic healing services.

The rite of exorcism — driving evil spirits out of a person by means of prayer and special rituals — survives today only as a part of the Sacraments of Initiation. There is also a ritual in the Roman Ritual which a priest may perform only with the permission of a bishop. However, the practice of exorcism in the Church has a very long history, and we can assume that many of the victims who experienced healing suffered from combinations of physical, spiritual, and mental ailments.

3. As Constitutive of the Gospel

We come to the end of this survey with a conviction of the Church's abiding concern for the sick. Whether the remedy addressed their physical or spiritual needs, the Christian community has always had a conviction that caring for the sick is an essential requirement of Gospel living. It is an imitation of a prominent element in Jesus's ministry and a response to his specific teaching. It is a consequence of the unity which binds all persons in charity and calls on them to bear one another's burdens. It is a recognition that all other human goods depend, to some extent, on the health of the human body. As the Bishops of the United States put it in their Pastoral Letter on Health and Health Care, "For the church, health and the healing apostolate take on special significance because of the church's long tradition of involvement in this area and because the church considers health care to be a basic human right which flows from the sanctity of human life."[18]

Christian ministry to the sick has revolved around the two poles of combatting illness and of using it as an occasion of spiritual benefit for the sufferer. To cite the bishops again:

> Christians know that pain permeates the human condition. But they also know that God did not abandon us to helpless acquiescence in suffering. . . . since the limitations of the human condition impose a degree of suffering and ultimately death for all of us, those involved in the healing mission of Christ render a unique service by bringing a faith dimension to these crucial moments.[19]

The sick and the bereaved, their families, loved ones, and associates are often most open to God's action in their hour of suffering.

It is not easy for the Church to know how to "visit the sick" effectively in today's world, however. The imperative to care for the sick today is qualified by contemporary understandings of injury and illness and by the "commodification" of modern health care.

Part Two: Factors Which Qualify the Christian Imperative

1. Contemporary Understandings of Injury and Illness

As we saw above, Jesus modified the then-prevalent ideas of disease as caused by sin or as a punishment for sin: "The primary insight of the New Testament (regarding illness) is that disease and disease-bringing demons, even if they are permitted to act by God (Acts 12:23; 2 Cor 12:7ff) have to do with the power of hostile forces which oppose the rule of God (Mk 1:23f; 3:27)."[20] Jesus's opposition to disease is an opposition to these hostile forces. Through the ages, though, depending on how mysterious in origin various diseases were, how capricious their incidence, or how horrible their consequences, they have often seemed like visitations of the devil or trials or punishments from God. Even a benign God could be expected to allow "bad things to happen to good people," to quote a recent popular book title, if it led to an increase in faith or a conversion of life. In an incarnational worldview in which God is understood to act through natural causes, sickness as well as health may be regarded as part of God's plan of salvation for individuals and peoples.

This transcendent dimension is less and less recognized in popular culture today, however, as physical ills are explained entirely in terms of natural causes to be overcome by scientific and technological remedies. As the ethicist, Daniel Callahan, expresses it:

> Medicine (today) is perhaps the last and purest bastion of Enlightenment dreams, tying together reason, science, and the dream of unlimited human possibilities. There is nothing, it is held, that in principle cannot be done and, given suitable caution, little that ought not to be done. Nature, including the body, is seen as infinitely manipulable and plastic to human contrivance.[21]

Bodily injuries are accounted for by accidents, mechanical failures, lapses in attention, negligence, and random or purposeful violence. Illnesses are caused by genetics, environment, nutrition, viruses, and bacteria. (The only illnesses we are still tempted to view as "punishments for sin" are lung cancer and venereal disease.)

When the causes of sickness are entirely natural, the remedies are too. Health of mind or body is a question of access to scientific knowledge or technology. From this point of view, the

patient is a set of assorted organs and physical processes working as a homeostatic unity that can be regulated by such physical means as surgery, drugs, hormones, rest, diet, et cetera.
Health care is a technical process similar to repairing a ma-
chine. Just as you take your car to the garage periodically to
have the technicians fix it, you take your body to a clinic or
hospital to have the specialists work on it. Some bodies are like
Maytag washers that seldom need the services of a repairman,
while others — perhaps because of neglect or hard usage — seem
to need help quite often!

It is hard to believe that, as recently as the turn of the century,
diagnoses of many illnesses were conjectural, causes were un-
known, therapies were palliative or useless, and life expectan-
cies were little more than half what they are today. One doctor,
looking back on the inadequacy of the medicines he prescribed
at the time, said they were little more than "symbols of good
intentions."[22] Today, as the result of anesthesia, antisepsis, sophisticated diagnostic tools, genetic engineering, vaccines, and
drugs, every disease seems at least potentially preventable or
curable. In fact, we are particularly affronted by such ills as
cancer, diabetes, and birth defects, because they have so far re-
sisted our scientific efforts. We spend hundreds of millions of
dollars annually on research to overcome them, confident that it
is merely a matter of time before the scientific breakthroughs
which will enable us to prevent or cure them.

Sophisticated technology also reinforces the conviction that
health depends on access to complicated machines for diagnosis
and treatment. Electron microscopes, computerized tomo-
graphy scanners, magnetic resonance imagers, heart-lung machines, lithotripters, and lasers are some of the tools which we
expect doctors to have at their disposal as they treat us.

Such cultural arbiters as television and the movies regularly
reinforce the idea that health depends on dramatic actions by
health care professionals who need an array of medical and
technological tools to restore persons to health. And, pharma-
ceutical companies, purveyors of the "miracle drugs," regularly
spend millions on advertising and image-building, not only of
their products, but also of themselves as contributors to the
common good and a better life.

It is true that, even today, there are those who dissent from
this confidence in scientific medicine. There were earlier
strands of "therapeutic nihilism," that is, a tendency to discount
the efficacy of existing drugs and therapies. For example, the
Christian Science Movement, homeopathy, botanic medicine,
folk medicine, and lay healing were some of its nineteenth cen-

tury expressions.[23] In recent years, a new skepticism about the benevolent intentions of health care professionals and their institutions has surfaced, and a variety of legal safeguards, aimed at limiting medical autonomy and ensuring patients' rights, have emerged.[24] A related movement has attempted to "deinstitutionalize" the dependent and "demedicalize" critical life events, such as childbirth and dying. Recent interest in hospices, home births, and midwifery derives, at least in part, from a desire to escape professional dominance and the desensitizing environment of the hospital. The phrase, "holistic medicine," has come into prominence to designate wellness-oriented régimes of diet, exercise, and self care.

More recently, in the light of escalating costs, critics of modern health care have asked whether our use of hospitals and surgery has become excessive and whether much of our medical care makes any difference in the overall health of the society. Faced with the fact that vast sums of money are spent on heroic procedures to prolong life in dubious circumstances, the public is more and more inclined to wonder about the cost-benefit ratio of modern health care.

Despite these doubts about the efficacy of some modern techniques and therapies, however, the operative paradigm for health care is still almost total reliance on scientific remedies. Even among those whose vocations are oriented toward the transcendent dimension of human life, efforts to augment or integrate scientific health care with religious healing are peripheral to their ministry. Interest in bridging the gap between scientific health care and healing ministries lies outside the mainstream of either the scientific or religious professions. Morton Kelsey, a proponent of the restoration of a tradition of healing services in Christian communities, tells the story of a friend who was state commissioner of health in a large Eastern state. At his suggestion, a group of doctors and clergy were called together to discuss the whole subject of spiritual healing: "While the physicians on the whole were deeply involved in the discussion, the clergy who attended the meeting hardly treated the subject as a serious one."[25] The theologian, Stanley Hauerwas, remarks that the trust we once put in God we now put in medicine, even though we know less about medicine than we once thought we knew about God.[26]

2. The "Commodification" of Health Care

The more health care has come to be regarded as a service rendered by professional experts using expensive drugs and equipment, the more it has become a commodity to be bought and sold. And, until quite recently, the more sophisticated and complex it became, the more it was restricted to the hospital. Health care moved out of the home and the doctor's office in this century; prior to that time, the hospital offered no special advantage over the home, even as a venue for surgery. As we saw earlier, hospitals in the United States were begun as charitable and religious institutions for the poor. Those who had means were cared for at home. But, the professionalization of nursing, improved hygiene in hospitals, and the introduction of equipment which an individual doctor did not have or could not bring to a home setting, gradually made the hospital the preferred site for surgery and episodes of acute illness. Sociologist Paul Starr remarks:

> The hospital is perhaps distinctive among social organizations in having first been built primarily for the poor and only later entered in significant numbers and an entirely different state of mind by the more respectable classes. As its functions were transformed, it emerged, in a sense, from the underlife of society to become a regular part of accepted experience.[27]

As the hospital changed from a charitable hospice for tending the sick into a medical institution for their cure, education, clinical instruction, and research were added to its responsibilities: "As hospital care turned into a sizeable industry at the end of the nineteenth century, . . . an orientation to the market became much more profound and widespread, even in voluntary institutions."[28] The hospital had become a workshop for the production of health; its customers (patients) purchased room and board and various amenities and the services of trained and licensed professionals.

Did Catholic hospitals undergo the same re-orientation to market values? In order to maintain their religious and charitable mission, they found it increasingly necessary to adopt sophisticated business practices and organizational arrangements. Founded to serve specific immigrant populations, Catholic hospitals were always open to the general community. In fact, in some places they were responsible for general public services, for example, in communities in which the Catholic hospital was the sole facility: "In Rochester, MN, the Mayo brothers came to rely exclusively on a Catholic hospital, St. Mary's, even though neither they nor the majority of their patients were Catholic."[29] As the services rendered became more complex and costs rose, Catholic hospitals, like their counterparts, relied more and more on public funding and private pay (either out-of-pocket or through insurance). Catholic hospitals were rarely able to accommodate all, or even most, of the poor. Rather, they struggled, with other voluntary hospitals, to maintain their charitable mission. In this, they participated in the common effort of all private, voluntary hospitals whose fortunes rose and fell with the economy. During the Depression, they struggled to stay open; after World War II and the enactment of the Hill-Burton Bill in 1946, they expanded and built.

By and large, Catholic hospitals, to the extent they reflected on it, did not find the transformation into a "business" inconsistent with their religious mission. The latter was never identified wholly with service to the poor, but also included service to the needy of all socio-economic groups, out of motives of religious commitment and in an environment of respect for religious beliefs and practices.[30] The chief symbol of the religious culture of the Catholic hospital was typically the presence of religious sisters in administration, nursing, and support services throughout the hospital. Even when the number of sisters actually serving in the institution was quite small compared with the total number of employees, the sisters' visibility and the proximity of other sisters in residence nearby helped magnify their effective influence. Until fairly recently, the sisters remained outside the economy of the hospital, paying themselves only a small stipend rather than a regular salary; they were religious missioned to the hospitals, not employees hired by it.

As hospitals became businesses in the twentieth century, they also grew in organizational sophistication. Corporate structures multiplied to include holding companies with multiple profit-making and non-profit subsidiaries. To reflect this growing business orientation, the American Hospital Association renamed voluntary hospitals: formerly "non-profit," they were now "not-for-profit."[31] It was evident that, to carry on their mission, to fund capital expansion and the purchase of new technology, all hospitals had to generate an excess of revenues over expenditures. Hospitals were also aggregated into regional and national systems, with corporate office staffs to oversee such key functions as finance, insurance, quality performance, and, in the case of Catholic systems, mission effectiveness. The "delivery" of health care services in the United States today requires a complex system of production, distribution, and financing, employs millions, and consumes twelve per cent of the Gross National Product. Today, there are 599 Catholic hospitals with annual net patient revenues in excess of $25 billion; seventy-four per cent of these hospitals belong to one of the fifty-eight Catholic multi-institutional systems.[32]

The "commodification" of health ministry extends beyond the services of doctors and hospitals. Many health related services, such as psychological and even spiritual counselling, are available from professional practitioners for a fee: "spiritual" therapies become business transactions! People "shop around" for a counselor, a masseuse, a trainer, or a personal dietician, for health clubs, spas, and wellness centers. All of this reinforces the idea that wellness and recovery from health-related problems, such as obesity or smoking, are products to be purchased in the marketplace.

3. Retreat from "Visiting the Sick" as a Ministry

For most Catholics today, "visiting the sick" is not a significant ministry because they regard the sick as victims of misfortunes which can be largely overcome by scientific and technological remedies, health care as something to be purchased from doctors and other specialists and from hospitals, and pastoral services as occasional interventions to be administered as needed.

The "business" of Catholic health care involves vast sums of money and extensive bureaucracies. These factors distance it from the everyday experience of most Church members, including Church leaders. The diffusion of responsibility for access to, and quality of, health care among the government, insurance companies, employers, and providers further alienates Catholics from a sense of ownership or responsibility for this ministry. To most Catholics, the hospital does not have any meaning as a significant site of Christian evangelization or witness. In fact, many are indifferent to whether or not the hospital they use is under Catholic auspices, depending entirely on their doctors to make the determination of where they go for hospitalization.

For many Catholics, pastoral services to the sick are synonymous with access to the Sacraments which a parish priest or chaplain can "deliver" in a public or community hospital as well as in a Catholic one. Parish ministry to the sick consists of Communion calls to the sick by Eucharistic ministers and occasional communal celebrations of Anointing for anyone who wishes to participate. Prayers for the sick and bereaved are a regular part of Sunday liturgy, but prayers for healing specifically through divine power are common only among so-called charismatic communities.

The Church's social ministry does not often target the needs of the sick, despite the well-documented lack of health care experienced by a large segment of the population.[33] The sheer magnitude of the problem means a systemic solution is needed, one which seems beyond the reach of individual charity or even the corporate efforts of the Church.

In summary, ministry to the sick within the Catholic community has become marginal to the general consciousness. As a work of mercy, it has become professionalized and secularized and, hence, estranged from the riches of Biblical inspiration and Christian tradition.

Part Three: Recovering the Tradition: "Visiting the Sick" Today

Renewing the tradition of ministry to the sick in contemporary society and re-integrating it into the life of the Church depend on three understandings: (1) of the value and meaning of health; (2) of the diversity of healing ministries; and (3) of the role and obligation of the Christian in ministering to the sick. After touching briefly on each of these topics, I will conclude with some applications to individual Christians, to the local Church, and to the institutional network which the Church maintains.

Health is a great human good, but not an absolute one. Its value derives from the value of life itself: health enables one to pursue the perfection of human life in community. It enhances the opportunity for religious, moral, intellectual, and cultural development, for creativity and productivity, for commitment and relationship. But, lack of good health need not condemn one to a life of meaninglessness. All of us know persons who, in spite of—or even because of—poor health or diminished physical or mental capacities, have lived lives of personal dignity and integrity and contribution to others. (This view of the relative value of health contrasts to the sometimes frantic quest for health in society which leads to desperate measures, unwarranted expenditures, and the denial of death.)

Any definition of health must be multi-dimensional, reflecting the various capacities and relationships of human life. The words, "health" and "healing," are derived from the same Anglo-Saxon root from which we get "holiness" and "wholeness." Health connotes wholeness in all of the dimensions of human life: physiological, psychological, mental, spiritual, ecological, social, et cetera. It likewise connotes freedom from conditions which would compromise well being in any dimension; namely, from disease, injury, hereditary defect, malnutrition, violence, oppression, loneliness, guilt, and habits of sin. It is not our purpose here to analyze all of the factors which constitute the fullness of health, but to point out that sickness — the absence of health — is similarly multi-faceted. Furthermore, perfect health is an abstraction: both wellness and sickness are on a continuum and relative to what is perceived as ideal.

It follows from this view of health and sickness that the healing ministries must be diverse and complex. As the theologian Bernard Cooke puts it: "There is a wide spectrum of activities that can fit under the canopy of 'healing': physical medicine, psychological therapy, spiritual direction, sacramental anointing, forgiveness of sins, and the reuniting of opposing social groups."[34] Effective healing requires the cooperative interaction of professionally trained persons in many fields, as well as the commitment of all members of the Church to assume some responsibility for this work of mercy, in ways appropriate to their knowledge, skills, and circumstances.

We spoke in Part One about the prominence of healing in the ministry of Jesus and in the life of the early Christians. This tradition has inspired the Church to use the metaphor of "doctor" or "healer" to describe the pastoral work of Jesus and his followers.[35] (Recall the words in Mk 2, "Those who are well do not need a physician.") The image has been used in many contexts and circumstances, e.g., Augustine of Hippo describes Christ as "the complete physician of our wounds." The *Apostolic Constitutions* compare the bishop to a doctor: "Heal, O bishops, like a compassionate physician, all who have sinned and employ methods that promote saving health." Sacraments, particularly Penance, are often described in medical terms. For the Council of Trent, the confessor is a "doctor of souls."

Imaging a Christian minister as a "doctor" can be very limiting if it implies only an essentially private, doctor-patient relationship. However, it is a very rich image if we open it out to the dimensions of knowledge, wisdom, and art which are sometimes attributed to the role of a doctor. "Doctor" connotes professional knowledge and excellence in service of human need. In many cultures, the doctor is a wisdom figure, a shaman, a medicine man, in short, one who has more than technical knowledge to bring to bear on the human condition. And, finally, "doctor" can connote skill in the "art" of diagnosis and healing. The Church's ministry of healing must employ similar qualities in service of the wide variety of "illnesses" which call for response.

Ministry to the sick is an activity of the "eyes," "heart," "hands," and "head." The first obligation is to *see* the sick, to observe the needs of our neighbors in all of their various forms. In some way, we must *feel* their anxiety, fear, and pain and be moved to compassion. Addressing the needs of the sick among us requires a combination of *personal effort* and *organizational response*. "Visiting the sick" cannot be entirely delegated to others, even though many maladies require professional knowledge and skill. There are sick among us, if we but see them, who call out for a consoling word, a soothing touch, some practical assistance. Moreover, the needs of those beyond our personal reach or capability require a variety of structural responses.

1. An Individual Commitment

Our individual commitment to this work of mercy begins with the conviction that Jesus calls us to care for the sick as part of our Christian identity. The Good Samaritan poured oil on the wounds of the man left by the side of the road *and* provided for continuing care by an innkeeper. Personal care and organized efforts, as reflected in this familiar story, are both part of the Christian responsibility.

The individual's obligation begins with care for his or her own health. As the bishops remark in their Pastoral Letter on Health and Health Care, we show respect for our own life and dignity when we adopt life styles that enhance our health and well-being and when we reject personal habits which threaten our health.[36] Caring for family members in episodes of acute illness or conditions of chronic illness is a common experience and obligation. Caring for the mentally retarded, the physically handicapped, or the senile can be a special demonstration of this work of mercy. Sharing the responsibility within a family can be a means of bonding together and a powerful witness to Christian compassion.

The sick themselves are called to be more than passive recipients of the ministry of others: "The role of the sick in the church is to remind others not to lose sight of the essential or higher things and so to show that our mortal life is restored through the mystery of Christ's death and resurrection."[37] The sick can teach us the way to cope with pain without self pity, the way to accept dependence on others without loss of dignity, the way to reassess our personal goals and priorities in the light of eternity. They can verify by their example the truth of the words of St. Paul: "We do not lose heart, because our inner being is renewed each day even though our body is being destroyed at the same time. . . . We do not fix our gaze on what is seen but on what is unseen. What is seen is transitory; what is unseen lasts forever" (2 Cor 4:16-18). By their suffering, the sick can be more intimately united to Christ, filling up what is lacking in his sufferings for the sake of the Church (Col 1:24).

Assisting the sick to prepare for death is a special pastoral privilege and responsibility. To be with the dying in their last hours is a salutary reminder of one's own vulnerability and finality. Encouraging their faith, supporting their struggles, assisting them to prepare for and celebrate the Sacraments of Penance, Anointing, and Eucharist — all of these are sacred duties of a Christian for another.

A great number of people are employed in the provision of professional health care, either in direct patient services or in supporting roles. Some, no doubt, are indifferent to the ministerial potential of their work, but others are aware of this dimension and make an explicit commitment to care for the sick as part of their Christian vocation. Their work becomes a work of mercy because of the understanding and intentionality they bring to it. One of the challenges which face leaders in Catholic health care institutions and agencies is to inspire all of the employees to be agents of Christian healing, "workers of mercy," whatever their religious affiliation.

2. The Local Church

Individual efforts to care for the sick need to be supported and augmented within the local Christian community, both the neighborhood or parish and the diocese. A number of practical examples come to mind. For example, the preparation of clergy and other ministers needs to give specific attention to the visitation of the sick, not only in the sense of pastoral care, but also of solicitude for their total health and well being. The Church need not, and cannot, be the provider of every kind of health care, but we need to see the individual's spiritual needs in the context of the whole person and to be attentive to assisting him or her to obtain needed services. Sunday homilies should help produce within the community a consciousness of the sick among us and an environment of mutual concern and assistance. They should promulgate the message that all of us are in some way in need of healing and that all have an obligation to help others. Opening the Word of God to the message of Christ's healing should inspire a recovery of this dimension of the Christian vocation.

Person-to-person ministry within the parish should be stimulated and coordinated, e.g., visits to the sick, the elderly, the homebound, the bereaved. Where this is done well, it has deep ramifications for the quality of Christian community. In today's single-parent or dual career families, time is at a premium, and a visit to a "stranger" can seem like an impossible demand, but helping others to make time for it is a task of pastoral leadership. Involving children in visiting the sick can be a powerful way of introducing them to the meaning of the Gospel. A visit to the sick can accomplish many things: alleviate loneliness, provide personal care, assist with household chores. But, at the heart of a visit which is truly a work of mercy is the moment where faith encounters faith and where something of God's love is revealed and God's work is done. It may be in a prayer, in a few words exchanged, in the quality of presence, one to another. The Rite for Visitation of the Sick makes some suggestions for Scriptural texts, special prayers, and ritual gestures, such as blessing with holy water. There are times when the formality of the visit or the imminence of death makes these appropriate, but any "visit to the sick" should include some dimension of faith encounter.

The communal celebration of the Sacrament of Anointing can sensitize the community to the needs of their neighbors, challenge them to service, and invite them to pray for others.[38] Even when the Sacrament is conferred on only one person, it should be in the context of a communal prayer service, to underscore the ecclesial dimensions. Parishes today commonly schedule celebrations of the Sacrament during a Sunday liturgy at intervals throughout the year. Where this is done, the whole service — Scripture readings, homily, music — should be developed around the idea of the consolation faith offers for those who are sick, the meaning of suffering and the hope of resurrection in human life, et cetera.

Recognizing that many persons suffer from the lack of access to basic health care services and that poor health compromises other basic human goods, such as ability to get an education or to work, we should give health care issues a prominent place in the Church's social agenda. Extension of insurance coverage to the poor and underserved and financial support for those with special needs ought to be priorities. Efforts of advocacy should mobilize citizen action at parish and community levels for maximum impact on public opinion and policy makers. Through the aegis of the local Church, the poor and most vulnerable should be empowered to speak out for their own needs.[39]

The Catholic Church has traditionally witnessed to its concern for the sick by providing an array of agencies and institutions for their care. As we noted above, these often seem remote from the life of the local Church today. This bond needs to be re-established by reaching out from both directions — the local Church leaders to the institutions and vice versa. The Catholic institutional network itself is scandalously fragmented and competitive within itself. With this problem in mind, the Commission on Catholic Health Care Ministry called on local Churches and/or regional groups to identify "needed but vulnerable institutions and programs, underserved and overserved populations, collaborative arrangements to provide a continuum of services in each service area, and maximization of opportunities for economies of scale."[40] The goal of this coordination is to produce a sense of shared responsibility for a common ministry within the Church.

Finally, the renewal of ministry to the sick requires leadership. To cite the Commission again:

> The goal of church leadership should be to engage the energies of the whole community in ensuring the availability of a spectrum of needed services, oriented toward the promotion of human well-being, accessible to the needy, and utilizing the resource of church members, families, and parish communities. The achievement of this goal will require initiative and support from many levels: parish, diocese, and national.[41]

Some Church agencies and institutions will have to sacrifice their individual preferences and even their autonomy to achieve the goal of a unified ministry.

3. The Institutional Network

A certain skepticism about the relevance of sponsored institutions is common in the Church. Catholic schools were victims of it in the 1960s, when the number of religious declined and tuitions were raised to pay for salaries to lay teachers. Schools continue to be important to a significant percentage of Catholic parents, but they are no longer so central to the identity of a Catholic parish as they once were. With regard to hospitals, we have already alluded to the indifference of many Catholics to their existence and to the lack of integration of hospitals into the mission of the local Church.

The Church originally established health care facilities[42] where none existed, in order to respond to the unmet needs of local communities. As the modern welfare State developed, the government assumed responsibility for supplying hospitals. At the same time, proprietary institutions were developed by doctors and other entrepreneurs. In recent years, the "commodification" of health care has included the development of large investor-owned chains. Given the existence of these facilities, should the Church continue to commit resources to sponsoring institutions, maintaining, as it were, a parallel system? The answer is, I believe, that we do not need all of the institutions we have today, but that the continued existence of some high quality ones under Catholic auspices is of tremendous value, for at least three reasons.

First of all, the Catholic health care facility gives public witness to the Church's commitment to *diakonia*, to preaching the Gospel in deed as well as in word. The institution's preference for the poor, or for those whose needs are otherwise unmet, should be a matter of public knowledge. The Catholic hospital can never care for all, or even most, of the poor, but it should be a conspicuous champion of their rights and creative in designing programs and services to assist them. The Catholic hospital is most effective when it coordinates and supplements the efforts of the many parishes, groups, and agencies in the local Church, thus contributing to a unified mission.

Secondly, the Catholic presence in health care is an opportunity for moral leadership. In her history of American hospitals, Rosemary Stevens concludes that, despite their orientation to business, what hospitals do has never been seen purely as a business; hospitals have always carried strong elements of idealism: "They are still, to some extent, . . . institutions through which the moral values of American society are expressed."[43] This is nowhere more true than it is in the Catholic hospital. An Episcopalian priest recently described Catholic hospitals to me as the conscience of modern health care. The ethical issues dealt with in health care are numerous and growing in complexity by the day. Examples are the uses of surgery and technology, human experimentation, genetic engineering, patients' rights, rationing of resources, prolonging life, managing pain, and a host of others. The Catholic hospital is a forum in which these questions can be examined practically as well as theoretically. Indeed, the Church's credibility in speaking to some medical-moral issues rests in part on its commitment to dealing on a day-to-day basis with suffering persons. The Catholic hospital develops a cadre of informed and inquiring professionals, a community of knowledge and care, within which it can examine some of the most pressing issues.

Thirdly, the Church's advocacy in areas of public policy is strengthened by the knowledge, experience, and corporate strength which its health care ministry provides. It is sometimes noted that the most pressing problems of modern life require systemic solutions. The need to reform our national health care system is one of the greatest problems facing the United States today. The Church has the opportunity and obligation to give moral leadership to the national debate, in part because of its participation in the system. With regard to advocacy, the Commission on Catholic Health Care Ministry said:

> Focused priorities, clearly articulated and successfully communicated at local, state, and national levels, will help the church — as an institutional presence and as a community of believers — effectively influence the social and political environment and advocate changes in the U.S. health care system.[44]

The Commission also noted that some of the issues which will call the whole Church to support a unified direction include extension of health care coverage, improved access to services, just distribution of resources, the application of new technology, and the empowerment of health care recipients.

The viability of the institutional health care ministry depends on the leadership of knowledgeable and committed laity. The recruitment and development of these leaders is one of the biggest challenges facing the Catholic health care systems today. A related issue is the need to develop new models of sponsorship which will insure the integrity and continuity of the mission when the religious congregations are no longer able to do so. Efforts to develop leadership and new models of sponsorship are in process; the next decade or so will reveal whether or not they will be adequate to preserve the institutional ministry into the next century.

* * * * *

Returning to the questions with which we began, what is the meaning of sickness and of health, and what is the purpose of our "visit" in today's world, we might respond as follows.

Sickness is the relative lack of health in some dimension of human life. It is a great evil, but not an absolute one, just as health is not an absolute good. Because of the unity of the human person, any diminishment in one aspect of the body or spirit affects the whole person. While sickness can be attributed to a variety of natural causes, it cannot be reduced to a mechanical failure to be remedied with merely scientific or technological means. Sickness is accompanied by pain, by loss, by a sense of vulnerability. It can be an opening to the power of God acting through the compassionate ministry of another.

Caring for the sick means addressing the needs of the whole person with a variety of healing arts and skills. This ministry is an integral component of the Christian vocation, both for individuals and for the local Church. It flows from the example and teaching of Jesus and from the long tradition of the Church. The institutional health care ministry adds a dimension of corporate service and public witness to this work of mercy.

The renewal of "visitation of the sick" requires a deeper understanding of its meaning and a recommitment to individual and corporate response.

NOTES

[1]Commission on a Catholic Health Care Ministry, *Catholic Health Ministry: A New Vision for a New Century* (Farmington Hills, MI, 1988), 1.

[2]Joachim Jeremias summarizes the critical studies in *New Testament Theology* (New York: Charles Scribner's Sons, 1971), 86-92. Joseph Champlin notes that almost one fifth of the Gospel text is given over to Christ's healings and to discussions prompted by these cures. He lists and classifies all of the incidents in *Healing in the Catholic Church* (Huntington, IN: Our Sunday Visitor, Inc., 1985), 35-39.

[3]Leonhard Goppelt, *Theology of the New Testament* (Grand Rapids, MI: William B. Eerdmans Publishing Co., 1981), vol. 1, 152.

[4]Ibid., 132.

[5]F. Graber and D. Muller develop the idea of Jesus' healing as a fulfillment of the Isaian prophecy, "It was our infirmities that he bore, our sufferings that he endured" (Is 53:4): "In taking up the cause of the helpless, Jesus proves himself to be the Servant of God (Mt. 8:17)." See "therapeuo," in *The New International Dictionary of New Testament Theology*, ed. Colin Brown (Grand Rapids, MI: Zondervan Publishing House, 1978), vol. 3, 165.

[6]This historical summary is indebted to E. Nasalli-Rocca, "The Christian Hospital to 1500," *New Catholic Encyclopedia* (Washington, DC: The Catholic University of America, 1967), vol. 7, 159-63.

[7]L. Butler, "Hospitallers and Hospital Sisters," *New Catholic Encyclopedia*, vol. 7, 155-58.

[8]Ibid., 161.

[9]For a fuller treatment, see A. B. McPadden, "The Christian Hospital: 1500 to the Present," *New Catholic Encyclopedia*, vol. 7, 163-66.

[10]This history is detailed in *Pioneer Healers: The History of Women Religious in American Health Care*, ed. Ursula Stepsis, CSA, and Dolores Liptak, RSM (New York: The Crossroad Publishing Co., 1989).

[11]Of the 263 sponsors of Catholic healthcare, more than eighty percent are congregations of women religious. According to the Catholic Health Association of the United States in *Catholic Health World* 6:23 (December 1, 1990), 2, there are presently 212 congregations of women, 37 dioceses, nine congregations of men, and five "other" groups sponsoring Catholic hospitals.

[12]The history of the rite is given by Jean-Charles Didier, *Death and the Christian* (New York: Hawthorn Books, 1961), 32-41, and Charles W. Gusmer, *And You Visited Me: Sacramental Ministry to the Sick and the Dying* (New York: Pueblo Publishing Company, 1984), 3-47.

[13]John F. Clarkson, S.J., et al, *The Church Teaches* (St. Louis, MO: B. Herder Book Co., 1955), 831-38; Gusmer, 34.

[14]The relevant text is James 5:14-16: "Is there anyone sick among you? He should ask for the presbyters of the church. They in turn are to pray over him, anointing him with oil in the Name (of the Lord). This prayer uttered in faith will reclaim the one who is ill, and the Lord will restore him to health. If he has committed any sins, forgiveness will be his. Hence, declare your sins to one another, and pray for one another, that you may find healing." Note that the text assigns responsibility for anointing to the presbyters — which was not the practice in the early Church. It was the fifth century before the Church made any definite connection between this text and the ritual. It seems that it was the rite and the Church's tradition which threw light on the text, rather than vice versa. Cf. Didier, 30-31.

[15]International Committee on English in the Liturgy, 1982. This is a translation, expansion, and adaptation of the *Ordo Unctionis Infirmorum eorumque pastoralis curae* of the Roman Ritual promulgated by Pope Paul VI on December 7, 1972.

[16]William A. Clebsch and Charles R. Jaekle, *Pastoral Care in Historical Perspective* (New York: Jason Aronson, 1975), 8.

[17]Ibid., 35-41.

[18]*Health and Health Care: A Pastoral Letter of the American Catholic Bishops* (Washington, D.C.: United States Catholic Conference, 1981), 3.

[19]Ibid., 19.

[20]"Nosos," in *The New International Dictionary of New Testament Theology*, 989.

[21]Daniel Callahan, *Setting Limits: Medical Goals in an Aging Society* (New York: Simon & Schuster, 1987), 60.

[22]Cited by Edward Shorter in *The Health Century* (New York: Doubleday, 1987), 4.

[23]Paul Starr, *The Social Transformation of American Medicine* (New York: Basic Books, Inc., 1982), 47-54, 93-99.

[24]Ibid., 390-3.

[25]Morton T. Kelsey, *Psychology, Medicine & Christian Healing* (San Francisco: Harper & Row, 1988), 3.

[26]Stanley Hauerwas, *Naming the Silences: God, Medicine, and the Problem of Suffering* (Grand Rapids, MI: William B. Eerdmans Publishing Company, 1990), 36.

[27]Starr, 145. The author gives an excellent summary of the development of American hospitals on 154-62.

[28]Ibid., 148.

[29]Ibid., 175.

[30]Service to the poor was only part of the reason for the founding of Catholic hospitals. Some were organized in response to discrimination against ethnic and religious minorities in the local public hospitals. For example, Massachusetts General Hospital initially refused to admit Irish patients on the grounds that their presence would deter other patients from entering the hospital (Starr, 173). Catholic hospitals offered Catholics some assurance that they would have access to the Sacraments, and they provided Catholic doctors a place for internships, residencies, and staff appointments when they were discriminated

against or excluded from other facilities. As their socioeconomic status improved, Catholics also came to look on their hospitals as a focus for their volunteer efforts and charitable giving and as a source of communal identity.

[31]Rosemary Stevens, *In Sickness and in Wealth: American Hospitals in the Twentieth Century* (New York: Basic Books, Inc., 1989), 285.

[32]Cited in the *1988-89 Annual Report of the Catholic Health Association of the United States* (St. Louis, MO, October 1989).

[33]Current estimates are that there are thirty-seven million Americans who are uninsured, including about twelve million children. Another twenty-two million have inadequate coverage.

[34]See *Ministry to Word and Sacraments: History and Theology* (Philadelphia: Fortress Press, 1980), 400.

[35]Regis A. Duffy, O.F.M., *A Roman Catholic Theology of Pastoral Care* (Philadelphia: Fortress Press, 1983). Chap. 3 deals with "The *Medicus* Symbol of Pastoral Care."

[36]*Health and Health Care*, 6.

[37]*Rite of Anointing and Pastoral Care of the Sick*, xi.

[38]Duffy, 97.

[39]Commission on Catholic Health Care Ministry, 20.

[40]Ibid., 19.

[41]Ibid., 18.

[42]This discussion of health care facilities includes institutions for the chronically ill and disabled and for the elderly, as well as clinics, social service agencies, acute care hospitals, et cetera. The question becomes the most acute for the latter, however, because of their high cost and complexity.

[43]Stevens, 364.

[44]Commission on Catholic Health Care Ministry, 15.

Index of Persons

AAN-8577